SIGN THE SPEECH

AN INTRODUCTION TO THEATRICAL INTERPRETING

JULIE GEBRON

Butte Publications, Inc., Hillsboro OR

SIGN THE SPEECH:
An Introduction to Theatrical Interpreting

© 1996 Butte Publications, Inc.
PO Box 1328, Hillsboro, OR 97123

Editing by Jean Miller and Glenn Williams
Design and graphics by John Plymale
Author photo by Mount Burns

ISBN 1-884362-04-4

Acknowledgements

There are always people to thank because theatrical interpreting, or any involvement in theatre, is a shared experience. This is a thank you to everyone I have ever worked with in theatre who has welcomed theatrical interpreting and been excited about all the creative and social/community opportunities it provides. From ushers to stage crew, incredible stage managers, actors who were eager to share the stage and worked hard to connect directly with all audience members, to box office folks, directors, audiences and teachers. A thank you to all the kids who attend shows and write letters afterwards asking for next year's schedule. To other interpreters who have provided feedback and support along the way, thanks.

Some special thanks as well to a very patient and supportive publisher, Matt Brink and to John Plymale for making layout and design a fun and survivable experience. To some wonderful interpreters I have worked with over the years (which means we sure have been through a lot together), Jean Miller, Tammy Fischer and Lisa Plymale... thanks for stressing, laughing, and still being excited about theatre. An overdue thank you to Gary O'Brien and Hank Stack who somehow convinced a very reluctant me to return to theatre as an interpreter. To Rebecca Lowe and Glenn Williams for all the creative energy, enthusiastic support and mostly for just plain "getting it" — thank you. And for my husband, Mount Burns, thank you — just because.

Contents

TRANSLATION PROCESS

TECHNICAL CONSIDERATIONS

CONCLUSION

APPENDICES

GLOSSARY

Introduction

This book is a beginning. It is written to provide basic information on the art of interpreting for theatre. It is one person's view of the requirements and processes of interpreting for the stage. It also presents a philosophy about theatrical interpreting. It is my view, based on my own experience as an interpreter, and as an actor who uses voice — but more often sign language — to present stories.

There are many perspectives on the value of interpreting theatre for audiences who are deaf or hard of hearing. Some folks think it is wonderful while others think it is worthless. The former believe it provides an opportunity to access theatre, the latter may tell you it does not involve Deaf people in theatre, but rather provides limited access to "Hearing" theatre and also pollutes Deaf theatre style. There are many others who sit somewhere on the line between these two extremes.

The reality is this: theatregoers who depend on sign language to access the dialog of a play have different needs, different interests, different experiences and upbringings. At one performance there will be people who are culturally Deaf, Hard of Hearing, Late-Deafened or Oral. There will be folks with extensive knowledge of theatrical works and kids attending for the very first time. There will be people with an interest in acting, and others who just love to sit in the audience and watch.

As a theatrical interpreter you are providing access. The people who want to attend a "hearing" play with sign language interpreters/actors will be at shows all the year round. Teachers will bring their students, parents will bring their children, families and couples — a blend of deaf and hearing — will share the experience together.

Is it the perfect situation? No. It is also not Deaf cultural theatre. It is a window into "hearing" culture. It shares art which is common knowledge in the Hearing world, or expresses political views or simply makes folks laugh. It is a new art form which is evolving. The more opportunities for access to the arts, the more exposure. The more people are exposed, the more they are inspired to create. With additional access, the presenters and the audience begin to meet each other and instead of two separate communities, they begin to work together. The fear and hesitation on the part of theatres to work with "disabled" actors dissipates. Familiarity breeds possibilities. As audience members attend and are given an opportunity to provide feedback (and that opportunity is always there simply by writing a letter or making a phone call) new ideas are considered. And sometimes, with the right combination of people, places and time, great things happen.

In the course of several years, one theatre company went from interpreters on the sidelines to shadow interpreted performances utilizing the skills of four interpreter/actors. They also taught some of their actors to sign their own lines. The same company began to hire Deaf consultants, then provided an opportunity to intern on stage during signed performances, then chose to cast a deaf person in a leading role. They expanded their volunteer opportunities, provided information and school visits to residential programs, and opened their doors to deaf actors and interpreters.

Another reality? There are very few Deaf actors, and those with a great deal of experience and teaching skills are often living in major metropolitan areas because that is where there are more opportunities to work. For those who live in smaller metropolitan areas, "hearing" theatre might be all there is right now. But through local theatres providing access by sign language interpretation, we provide an opportunity for someone to be inspired by the idea of live theatre. Inspiration may come in the form of delight at the prospect of performing live on stage, or may come in the form of anger and frustration! Perhaps someone in the audience will hate watching a show via interpreters, or even dislike what they consider to be a "hearing" theatre style which does not satisfy their needs for enjoying a play. Great! They may be motivated to take action and create what they feel is needed. Whatever their response, they had the opportunity to respond.

As a theatrical interpreter, you are there to provide the best possible performance, giving the maximum amount of access under the limitations placed upon you by the theatre. You are also there to educate the people who work in theatre. You are there to create opportunities: at times, merely by your presence providing the awareness that there are many different folks out there, with many different hearing abilities, language styles and backgrounds. And they are all, for one moment, sitting in the same space together because they want the emotional experience of participation which live theatre brings: an experience which is different for every single person in that audience; an experience which, for some people, will be enhanced by your performance.

Theatre is a continually evolving, often controversial journey which inspires everyone who participates. At its best, it makes people think and it makes them confront who we are as a society—both on stage and in the audience. As a theatrical interpreter you will travel on this journey. There are no maps, not even a destination. There is very little to guide you.

This book is a start.

1. Getting Started

There are a lot of people who interpret theatre productions, and a lot of folks who would like to become more involved in this specialized art of interpreting. But there are some important questions to ask yourself before you take the plunge. Theatre work is unlike any other interpreting assignment. Anyone who stands in front of an audience to present a production is an artist, an actor, a performer. What a performer strives for is the presentation of a vision (a stage picture) which is usually determined by a director in collaboration with other theatre artists. The signing performer must recognize, understand and work with that vision. A love for the theatre is necessary. An awareness that this is, above all, not just an interpreting assignment, but rather, a performance, which requires immense research, time and preparation.

What is theatrical interpreting? It is a new art form. It is not merely translating words; it is creating a work of art. It is striving to re-interpret the director's vision and in the process creating a different stage picture of that vision. It is realizing that while there are many ways interpreters relate physically to the stage, they all require acting. It is acting, but it uses a different language and style to communicate the story.

A VERY BRIEF HISTORY

Historically, theatres who chose to provide interpreted performances would ask around to find the sign language interpreters in their area. Then they would call and ask the interpreter(s) to sign one or two performances of a production. Often, theatres would hire just one interpreter to sign a production, even though there might be ten or twenty characters in the show! The rehearsal process for the interpreter(s) usually consisted of watching one or two of the performances of a show. A copy of the script was sometimes provided, but not always. On the day of the sign interpreted performance, the interpreter(s) would arrive wearing all black, and would stand to the side of the stage, very far away from the actors, lit by a single bright light. (Sometimes the light would stay on the entire performance, even when the stage lights went to black. This choice often angers the members of the audience who are "hearing" as it disturbs the emotional value of a blackout.) This set up the notorious "ping-pong" effect for deaf audience members, who were forced to watch an interpreter far off to one side and then quickly turn their heads to look at the stage and catch some of the action.

Interpreters working under these conditions received little or no feedback during a rehearsal process and were not considered part of the production. They were more or less tacked on to a production already in existence. Usually, after the performance, hearing members of the audience would rave about the beauty of sign language and how wonderful it was that a theatre had offered this incredible experience to deaf and hard of hearing people.

While this may sound very archaic and oppressive, there are still many theatres who approach sign interpreted performances in this way. Many interpreters are hired at the last minute to sign for performances and given very little support by the theatre or touring company.

Fortunately, with education and the Americans with Disabilities Act (ADA), more theatres are beginning to understand how to provide true access. Theatres are hiring interpreters earlier, providing scripts and rehearsal schedules, improving the placement of interpreters and in many cases, experimenting with the incorporation of interpreters on stage during performances. That means, people who interpret for theatre need to be better prepared not only as translators, but as performers.

SOME CONSIDERATIONS

So here are some questions you should ask yourself. Why do you want to work in the theatre as a signing performer/interpreter? If it is viewed as a basic interpreting assignment, at which an interpreter arrives, signs the language heard and leaves at the conclusion of the performance, then perhaps this is not the most appropriate "assignment" to accept when offered. Let's face it, numerous theatres and touring companies have become aware of the need to provide interpreted performances and are notorious for calling every interpreter around to check on their availability and fee. You need to decide if the performance is an appropriate area for your skills and accept offers based on whether you are able to do the best job within the given parameters of time, fee and type of production. The decision should not be based on whether or not you can show up at the theater on the night of the performance!

Ask yourself again, why do you want to interpret for theatre? What is your perception of yourself as a member of the creative process? Are you an interpreter or an actor who happens to be fluent in sign language and uses that medium while performing on stage? It is the person who views him or herself as an actor who signs who will ultimately provide the best theatrical experience for the audience. To put it in plain and simple terms, working in theatre requires actors, not interpreters. Being a skilled, fluent, maximally certified interpreter does not mean you can get up on stage and perform because theatre requires much more than language translation skills.

BASIC QUALIFICATIONS

Interpreters who succeed in theatre are actors in their souls. They commit an immense amount of time and energy to the process of understanding the production as the director and cast have decided to present the work. They work on the translation of the text and language not as they perceive the meaning to be, but as the actors and the director intend the meaning. They understand the characters and the type of sign choices that fit the character as it is portrayed in a specific production. They know how to work with actors and directors and technical staff to enhance the production for all audience members.

Sign language interpreters, educational or freelance, do a better job interpreting when they are familiar with the information and/or have experience with the material needing to be interpreted. Interpreters need to comprehend information before they can translate.

Plays are written works. They are stories created to be acted on a stage. To be an excellent theatrical interpreter, you need to read. You need exposure to a wide range of literature, from classic works, to poetry, to liberal or diverse magazines such as *UtneReader, The Nation, Harper's Bazaar* or *The New Yorker*. Playwrights often include references to politics of the time, social mannerisms, protagonists and antagonists from great, and at times elusive, literary works. To translate words, context and meaning, you need to be familiar with the references the playwrights incorporate in their work. To interpret Shakespeare you need to know mythology and astrology, to be familiar with the Elizabethan perspective of the world. Shakespeare's plays present classic themes: good and evil, love, war, power, youth, age and ever-progressing time. His plays are language rich, the plots often dependent on layers of history, social mores, superstitions, religion and culture. And whether or not you choose to interpret Shakespeare, you still need familiarity with his works. Shakespeare is referenced again and again in classic and modern dramas.

You don't need to spend a lot of money on books and magazines. If you want to be able to write in the margins and make notes, or if you know you will use a book frequently, then buy it. Otherwise, borrow what you need from the library.

To understand much of what you will translate for theatre, you need reference materials. A good dictionary and a thesaurus are a start, but you would also benefit from books that explain specific events, places or eras represented in a play. Suppose a play based in the 1950's mentions a specific type of car. You could generically sign CAR, but if that specific model was central to the story, you should know what the car looks like. And why is it special? For example, the musical *Grease* includes a song entitled

"Greased Lightnin." The song describes the dream car of one of the characters, using phrases such as "palamino dash board" "dual muffler twins" and "overheard lifters". The song itself provides a terrific opportunity for a fun visual translation into ASL, but you need to know what the heck is being described! To help us with the translation, we asked a man familiar with cars from the 1950's and also looked in a visual dictionary.

Foreign language dictionaries are also useful. There are many characters in English language plays who throw in some Latin or French or Spanish. Sometimes the playwright assumes the phrase is so common that a footnote is not needed to explain the meaning. That's when a foreign language dictionary can be a tremendous help.

Sign language books are helpful. Not just modern texts, but older texts which often include signs in their older two handed form. When signing a play set near the turn of the century, signs can be used in their older but still recognizable form to convey the language choices made in the written English text which reflects vocabulary particular to the period of the play.

Since you will be interpreting theatre productions, you should attend as much theatre as possible. This doesn't mean to limit yourself to sign language interpreted performances only. You need to familiarize yourself with the craft of theatre. You need to see the works of famous playwrights, watch the actors and their characterizations, hear the language, take in the sets and costumes. You need to immerse yourself in theatre, just as you immersed yourself in another culture as you trained to be an interpreter.

You might take some classes relating to theatre, dance, improvisation and movement. Theatre appreciation classes often include attending a variety of plays, with class discussion afterwards.

Network with other interpreters interested in theatre, either living in the same area or connect on line.

Other basic qualifications include:
- Language fluency in ASL, English and MCE
- Excellent translation skills - interpreting for meaning and context, not just vocabulary
- A respect for the creative process
- Acting/Performance skills and experience
- Knowledge of theatre terminology
- The ability to analyze plays and other written works
- Flexibility - physical and mental
- Physical stamina (You may be interpreting for a two hour show without an intermission!)
- Commitment, or in other words, the ability to work long hours for little pay
- The ability to work cooperatively with individuals and groups in the creative process
- Good decision-making skills (Don't interpret what you don't want to interpret, or works you don't understand.)
- A lot of time in the evenings for rehearsals and performances

You need to be a good communicator, able to listen and learn, willing to leave your insecurities at the door and eagerly join the world of theatre.

The more exposure you have to the world of theatre, the better your understanding of each production you interpret.

MAKING THE DECISION

Suppose you are called by a theatre to interpret performances of an upcoming production. Here are some of the questions you need to ask before you can make a decision to interpret/perform in the production.

First, it's a good idea to know which show is being produced. For example, if it is a musical comedy, is that something you have the skills to perform? Or if it is a play about a person who is gay, or racist, or if the show portrays violence — are those topics you feel comfortable interpreting? Many people agree to interpret for a performance and later realize that the subject matter makes them feel uncomfortable. If you are uncertain, request a script and read through the play before making a decision. If possible, you may want to chat with the director. Keep in mind however that the language of the play does not show how a director will choose to stage the production. A seemingly benign play you read may include a great deal of graphic and explicit action during production. It is most important that you feel comfortable with the topic of the play. It is equally important that you understand the language! If you do not understand Shakespeare, and you do not have the time to commit to learning what it all means and then figuring out how to express it in sign language, don't do it!

1) What are the dates the show will be interpreted?

2) How many accessible performances will be offered?

3) How much rehearsal time will be needed and when are rehearsals scheduled? You should accept performances that not only fit your schedule in terms of performance dates, but also allow you enough time to rehearse and prepare for the production. If you are scheduled to work everyday for the two weeks before a performance and are unable to rehearse in the evening on a regular basis due to other schedule constraints, then you do not have time to prepare for a show. Be realistic. Yes, it is fun to do shows, but if your schedule does not permit you to do a good job, then turn down the offer.

4) Where will the interpreters be during the performance? As far as placement, if the signers will be onstage during a production, many more hours of rehearsal will be required than platform interpreting work. Rehearsals are fixed appointments. If you are unable to attend the required rehearsals at the specific times scheduled, then you will probably not be working on that specific production. If you will be staying in one location throughout the performance, as is the case with platform interpreting, you will probably have the freedom to attend rehearsals that fit your schedule more conveniently. Equity theatre companies

often rehearse during the day, while non-union theatres usually rehearse evenings and weekends.

5) Once you have established that you feel comfortable with the type and content of the production, are available to perform and rehearse and also feel comfortable with the location of the interpreters during the play, you need to agree upon the payment amount and when payment will be made. Then you need to request certain items that will help you give a great performance.

WHAT YOU NEED FROM THE THEATRE COMPANY

Contract
It is very important you sign a contract with the theatre. The contract needs to state the dates of the performances which you will interpret, the amount you will be paid, when payment will be made, the amount of time needed by either party to terminate the agreement, your social security number, appropriate addresses and signatures. The contract may also specify benefits such as complimentary tickets, discounts on merchandise, dates of photo calls and whatever benefits the theatre company may choose to provide. *(See SAMPLE CONTRACT in the Appendix.)*

Scripts
The theatre company also needs to provide each interpreter with a complete script of the play. Ask that this is sent with your contract, or arrange to pick it up in person at the theater. At the same time, you can pick up a rehearsal schedule. Hopefully, you have been hired for a play before rehearsals begin!

Cuts
All script cuts need to be shared with the interpreters. If interpreters are attending rehearsals on a regular basis, cuts can be copied directly from the "production book", which is the most current version of the production. If the show is a touring production, contact the stage manager and ask for the most recent version. Shows on their way to Broadway cut and add lines on a

daily basis, so the last thing you want is a copy of the original script from their first performance!

Rehearsal Schedule

The rehearsal schedule lists the dates and times of the rehearsals. It also gives an outline of what will happen at each rehearsal. If you are shadow interpreting a performance, rehearsals integrating the signers into the performance should be noted on the schedule. When interpreter rehearsals are included on the printed rehearsal schedule, expectations are clear for actors and production personnel.

Access to rehearsals is necessary to ensure the best possible translation and performance. Periodic visits during the rehearsal process should be scheduled. Interpreters often rehearse at run-throughs and dress rehearsals. Shadow interpreted performances require blocking rehearsals.

Audiotapes

A recording of the show from start to finish including all music and/or other sound cues is one of the most valuable tools used by theatrical interpreters. The tape should be recorded at the first available opportunity, often an early run-through. A dress rehearsal is also a good time to tape. The tape is usually recorded by the sound technician, the stage manager or the assistant stage manager, but don't be surprised if you are expected to record your own tapes during a rehearsal. For Broadway touring shows, you will often be given a nationally distributed cast recording. Be sure to compare it with the most recently edited version of the script as there are often many differences. In addition, due to Equity and copyright restrictions, you may not be able to obtain an audiotape of musical productions which includes the spoken dialog! If this is the case, and you have a limited amount of time in which to prepare for the show, and if you are not familiar with the show and if there is not a film version which is similar to the stage production, you might not want to accept the job. It is extremely difficult to prepare for a performance for which there is no audiotape or videotape as it is important to hear the dialog during your rehearsal process. If there is not an accurate and complete audiotape available and you are able to attend many performances before you will sign the show, then it may be worth considering.

Music
Lyrics for all songs not appearing in the printed script should be given to interpreters with audiotapes of the music as it will be performed as soon as possible. Be especially on the lookout for pre-show, intermission or post-show music. The music director will have this information before anyone else!

Comps
These are "complimentary tickets" or "compensatory tickets" given to performers to help them prepare for the performance, and also as part of the contract agreement. Local theatres will almost always let you in to see a show as many times as you think necessary before your actual performance date. You are often given two or more comps to give to friends and/or family. Touring productions vary in the number of times you may watch a performance. Usually the stage manager will be very flexible about letting you in, while the promoter/producer will limit you to one viewing. The stage manager can arrange for you to sit in the technical booth, or enter through the Stage Door and be escorted to an empty seat in the theater. The promoter/producer has to account for every person walking in the front doors and cover the cost of their ticket.

Contact Sheet
This is the paper which lists the names and phone numbers for actors, designers, production crew (including stage managers and directors) and administrative numbers for the theatre. For local productions you need to have this information, or at least basic contact names and numbers for the production personnel.

Dressing Room
An assigned space for changing clothes and applying make-up is just as important for a signing performer as a speaking/ singing performer.

Programs and Lobby Signs

As a performer, you deserve recognition and credit for your work. If possible, your name should be included in the program or playbill distributed to the audience. Many theatres list the names of the interpreters on the same page as the cast list, indicating their presence only during signed performances. It is also likely that local theatre companies will print a bio (a brief summary of your theatrical interpreting and acting experience) as well as a head shot (a close-up photograph of your face) in the program.

For touring productions, or shows that hire you after the program is printed, recognition can be printed on an additional paper and inserted into the audience programs or playbills. Another option is to post a sign in the lobby that states "Tonight's performance will be interpreted into sign language by..." and then lists the names of the interpreters.

Bows/Curtain Calls

Theatrical interpreters are sometimes shy about taking their bows, but they definitely deserve the appreciation of the audience for their performance. A curtain call is also a courtesy to the audience as it gives them the opportunity to thank you for your hard work. The director or stage manager will determine the bow for the interpreters. Touring companies often take their own stage bows, then indicate the signers (who are usually platform interpreting below or to the side of the stage). Interpreters placed on stage either for zone or shadow interpreted performances may be specially indicated, or may bow with the ensemble. If you have not been given instructions about the bow, ask the stage manager for instructions before the performance.

It may be helpful to create a checklist to make sure you have all the information you need to provide an excellent performance with a minimal amount of stress. Remember, theatre interpreting is a specialized field requiring extra work and research. Take advantage of tools and opportunities to improve your qualifications. Once you are hired, be prepared and professional. Read the script, gather information from the director and stage manager and make your decisions. Now you are ready to begin!

EXAMPLES OF
BASIC INTERPRETER PLACEMENT
(based on proscenium stage)

X = Interpreter   **O** = Actor

PLATFORM OFFSTAGE

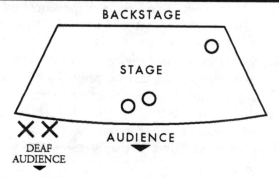

SIGHTLINE

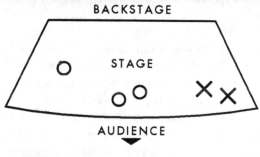

ZONE

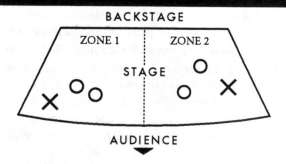

2. Placement of Interpreters

Where the interpreters will be placed during the performance makes a big difference in the rehearsal process, the stage picture and ultimately in the level of enjoyment by the audience. Usually, the closer the audience is to the actors, the better the level of enjoyment. But this intimate playing is more often the exception rather than the rule. If you are informed about the variety of placement options, and are creative as well, you may be able to participate in making the decision about where the interpreters will perform. Most of the time however, the decision will be made by the director, stage manager, producer or company manager before you even enter into the process.

EDUCATING THE DECISION MAKERS

There are opportunities for your knowledge about theatrical interpreting to be shared. As you continue to work in this specialized field, you will meet a variety of folks who have the authority to make or influence decisions about the placement of interpreters. Some of these people are very open to exploring new ideas, and may be willing to try different locations for interpreter placement. Find these people and make them your friends! Educate them about the wide variety of options and excite them with the creative possibilities offered by interpreted performances.

You also must realize that many people are offended by the idea of interpreted theatre and especially by placing the interpreters anywhere near the action. It is best to remain diplomatic, professional and friendly, rather than getting on a political soapbox. But when you find someone receptive to your ideas, work with that person cooperatively to enhance the placement of the interpreters. The earlier you are involved in the production process and are able to talk with people, the better chance that your ideas might be implemented. Most important is for you to be ready to educate the decision makers to help them make educated choices.

PLATFORM INTERPRETING

When a theatre decides to offer a sign interpreted performance, more than likely they envision one or two interpreters dressed in black, standing off to the side, either on the stage itself or in front of the apron. This type of placement is known as "platform interpreting." Basically, it requires the signers to stand or sit in one location for the duration of the performance. This is the preferred placement for most theatre companies because it is, from their perspective, the "least intrusive" method. This means several things. First, that the signers are not part of the stage picture, hence retaining the integrity of the director's vision. Second, the signers are not a "distraction" to the majority of the audience. Third, it is the least amount of work in terms of rehearsal time, lighting, and costuming. Fourth, it is less distracting to the actors.

There are obvious problems to this method. For the audience members who depend on the interpretation to enjoy the production, a choice must be made between watching the signers or the play. This creates the "ping-pong" effect for the audience, who must continually turn their heads towards the signers to catch the language (and hence the plot), then turn and watch the actors on the stage to see the action. The audience members needing sign language end up missing dialog and action because they must continually change their focus. Platform interpreting is also a distraction for hearing audience members as well. They will always watch the signers as well as the action, thus experiencing the "ping-pong" effect. It is a myth to think platform interpreting is less distracting.

Interpreters working in this situation need to make the choices which will enhance the enjoyment of the production. This is accomplished through a careful evaluation of the script and concentrated analysis of the action on stage. Striking stage pictures, moments with a great deal of action which clearly convey meaning, magic, special effects, set changes or grand entrances may not need to be signed at all. If it is a moment that is much more fascinating to watch and can be understood purely from the action on the stage, then the signers need to cue the audience to watch the stage. This is a matter of timing. It requires the signers to be finished with their signing before the moment occurs, so the audience has a chance to look at the stage and be prepared for the action. To cue the audience, the signers just return to a neutral body position, hands relaxed at their sides, and look towards the stage. Depending on the type of production, a cue might be more grandiose or even added to the script. For a comedy, the signers could make it into a fun cue, like a signed fanfare. A children's production might require the sign, LOOK, directed toward the stage. No matter how the cue occurs, it should fit with the style of the production. The signers should also look at the action on the stage. This lets the audience members know to watch the stage. When the signers face the audience again, this is a cue that signing will resume.

Another way to make the best of the platform situation is to choose when not to sign. Often, this will be during those moments on stage just dicussed, but there may be other times as well. At a performance of *The Illusion*, the director chose to begin the play in complete darkness. The only light came from a match, struck by one of the characters as he enters a cave. The character says "Hello" a few times and asks if anyone is there. From the actions of the character, the lighting of the match and his facial expression, it was obvious he was searching for someone in an unfamiliar place filled with mystery and power. I chose not to sign his few "hellos" and remain in darkness. Bringing the lights up for the interpreters to sign would completely destroy the effect of a single match illuminating the dark. The lines did not require interpretation, and the mood for the show was established during the entrance of the character. By not signing those few lines, the entire audience was able to feel the magic that was integral to the production.

Platform interpreters are usually lit by a single bright white light.

The lightboard operator in the technical booth will usually bring this light up or down with the stage lights. That means the light will not be on when the stage is dark. Sometimes the light is left on during the entire production, even when the stage is completely black for a scene change or effect. This means the audience can always see you. If you are fidgeting, or picking at your fingernails, or looking around for your friends in the audience, or even just looking bored, you will be observed by everyone in the house. For those reasons, a permanent light should be discouraged. It often happens simply because it is never discussed! During a performance, you are a performer, and should remain in character or in a neutral state whenever appropriate.

Entrances and exits should also be carefully considered when platform interpreting. Often the house lights will dim to half their original power, and then fade to black. The signers will usually move to their position during the blackout. If the platform area will be reached from within the house, rather than an entrance from the wings, the signers should get to a position near the platform when the house lights go to half. The location should be close enough to the platform to permit an easy, clear path to the signing area without being in front of the audience before the lights go to black. Most stage managers will make sure glow tape has been placed at strategic spots to guide the signers to the platform area. This should be discussed with the stage manager in advance as you will probably not have a chance to rehearse the show from the platform area. Since each theater has its own unique layout, the signers will need to work with the stage manager to figure out the best way to enter and exit.

At the end of the performance, the interpreters are usually acknowledged by the cast or asked to bow at the same time as the actors. The stage manager will make the decision about the bows, but may need to be reminded before the show. Stage managers experienced with sign interpreted performances often have everything organized and well under control. Still, reviewing your needs will make sure nothing is missed.

Because platform interpreters are further away from the action, it may be more difficult for the audience to distinguish which signer is portraying which character. Facial expression and characterization need to be more obvious. Sign choices should lean more towards two handed signs which can be held for a longer amount of time. This makes the signs larger and easier to read when looking back and forth between signers and the stage.

Platform interpreting is the most commonly used placement for theatrical interpreters, although it is not the most preferred.

SIGHTLINE INTERPRETING

Sightline interpreting is basically platform interpreting where the signers are placed a bit more strategically on or near the stage to allow the audience a better view of both the signers and the stage picture. For example, the signers might be placed standing or sitting in front of and below the stage. This should allow the audience members to look at the stage in nearly a straight line, with the interpreters in that line of vision. Deaf and hard of hearing patrons have the best view of the signers and the stage when seated at least four or five rows behind the front row. (Again, the seating plan for each theater space needs to be taken into consideration when designating seating for view of the signers.) Placement for a raised stage would most likely be on a platform directly below the stage and usually off to one side. This location would once again be illuminated by a single spot light. Some theaters have seats that look down on the stage, so that the first row is level with the stage. In this staging, interpreters might be placed on the stage or on a platform towards the back of the stage. In this case, the best viewing is from seats where the audience can see beyond the speaking actors heads to the signers behind.

Sitting on the edge of the stage is another option in theaters where the stage is at least several feet above the level of the front row. This is especially effective for children's shows where an intimate, storytelling atmosphere is appropriate.

ZONE INTERPRETING

Another placement option is known as "zone interpreting" (sometimes affectionally referred to as "zone defense"). This method places the interpreters in designated areas on the stage during the performance. The signers might be in stationary placements or on platforms, or the signers might be able to move about the stage within their individual zone. The concept behind this strategy is to place the interpreters as close as possible to the action on stage without a great deal of complicated blocking for the signers. When signers are allowed to move around the stage area, they are often directed to stay stage right or stage left of the action, consciously avoiding any placement that might block the rest of the actors on the stage.

Zone interpreting allows the signers to be closer to the characters, but usually keeps the signers at opposite sides of the stage. While there might be moments throughout the performance when the signers are near each other, often they are in separate areas. This means that the division of characters (who signs which lines) is based completely on movement of the actors. The signer closest to a character signs the lines. Even if there are four or five characters in the same zone, the interpreter closest to the action would sign all the lines. Suppose all the characters are blocked stage left, the stage right interpreter could move in closer to the group and pick up lines for the nearby characters. This could create a ping-pong effect for the viewers, if the signers are on each side of the speaking actors. If the signers are placed next to each other, or at least in a closer proximity, it will be easier for the audience to watch the show.

It is more difficult to rehearse for zone interpreting, as the blocking for the characters is subject to change as late as the final dress rehearsals. Every time the blocking is changed, the signers need to determine how this effects their blocking and choice of who will sign specific lines. Zone interpreting requires signers who are comfortable on the stage and can adapt easily to the movements of all the actors. The stage picture changes from the director's vision once additional people are added to the production.

That's why it is especially important that you look as comfortable on stage as the rest of the performers.

SHADOW INTERPRETING

Of the different methods for presenting a sign interpreted performance, shadow interpreting is the most challenging for everyone involved in the process. The payoff, however, is a production that is much more enjoyable for all audiences. Rather than several signers obviously "tacked on" to a performance, shadow interpreters are smoothly integrated into the complete production through costuming, placement, movement and signing style. The signers are placed as close as possible to the speaking actors, following the characters' blocking, and sometimes even their actions throughout the performance. This means, if the speaking actor kneels, the signer kneels. When the speaking actor crosses the stage, the signer also makes the same cross. The extent to which the movements and blocking of the speaking actor are "shadowed" by the signer varies depending on several factors which include: the type of show, the director's concept, the limitations of the stage and/or set, and the number of signers. When there are only two shadow interpreters for three or more characters during a scene, choices have to be made about the best placement of the signers. If numerous characters are scattered about the stage in separate locations, the signers locations could be next to the main characters. They might also be placed in the midst of several characters. The challenge will be to place the interpreters in locations that allow the audience to know which character is speaking, especially in scenes with a large number of characters.

Suppose the set is built with areas that are only large enough for one person, such as a window or balcony. A decision must be made about the placement of the signer that best allows the audience to see the actor and signer. In the case of a balcony, is there a nearby window that a signer could use? Perhaps the signer can stand under the balcony. Or could the actor in the balcony learn to sign their lines for that scene? Be creative when confronted with challenging set designs.

Shadow interpreting requires many more hours of rehearsal than either platform or zone interpreting because the signers must be blocked very specifically into the stage picture. In fact, the director basically needs to create two shows at the same time: one which includes signing performers and one without the signers. Some directors will be frustrated with the process, others will be thrilled to have an opportunity to work with a new art form. Directors have been extremely innovative when given the opportunity to create a second stage picture which includes the signers.

A show with many characters usually provides more options for integrating signers into the production than a show with two or three characters. With a larger cast, there are often more background characters such as servants, soldiers or just people on the street. When a show includes numerous background characters, signers can easily be integrated into the production because there are more options for characterization and placement. Signers have appeared as party-goers in a show set at a cocktail party, as store clerks, waiters, curious onlookers, prostitutes, members of a royal entourage, carpenters, magicians, narrators or manifestations of a character's imagination or conscience. For example, in *A Midsummer's Night Dream,* we blended in as fairies. Our costumes included fabrics similar to other characters, our make-up was fantastical and as fairies, we were able to freely move about the stage. We participated in simple dances, observed and commented on the "humans" and blended in with the other actors. For a production of *Hot L Baltimore,* we were dressed as lower class tenants of the hotel. We comfortably moved about the stage as if we lived there, sitting on the stairs or falling asleep on the couch.

The integration of interpreters into a production is limited only by the creativity of the people creating the signed performance. It all depends on the concept chosen for placing and integrating the signers into the production.

3. Theatre Savvy

The theatre world offers a great variety of venues in which you might provide sign interpretation for productions. Even if you only work with one specific theater over a period of time, there are aspects of basic theatre behavior, structure and terminology you should learn.

Theatres are usually non-profit organizations. This means they depend on donations, grants and corporate sponsorship for a large part of their income. Most theatre companies are run by a small number of full-time and part-time artistic and administrative staff, with consultants, designers, directors and actors hired in for each individual production. Because minimal staffing is often the case, each employee of the theatre is carrying more than their fair share of responsibilities. In plain and simple terms, you will be dealing with people who are frequently overworked and underpaid. They work in theatre because they love theatre, and for the most part, they do a remarkable job of keeping a complicated organization running smoothly with limited staffing.

In addition, most of these people have little or minimal information about sign language, interpreting and people who happen to be deaf or hard of hearing. You may be their first link to a whole new community. This means you will be once again in the familiar interpreter role of educator. You will need to be kind, respectful, professional and patient. Your contract might be late or a script might not be readily available. After all, when scripts were ordered, most likely no one thought to include the signers on the list of people needing scripts. Be flexible, be friendly, but also make sure you get what you need to prepare for your performance.

WHO'S WHO IN THEATRE

The Administrative Team

Who are the people you will meet? Even the smallest theatres tend to have an artistic director. This is the person who envisions and leads the artistic direction of the company. The artistic director oversees artistic aspects of production and design. The A.D. is often the person who selects which plays will be performed in a given season and hires the directors for each production. Auditions are usually coordinated and run by the artistic director. It is often this person who will determine how the theatre company will present sign interpreted performances. If you are fortunate enough to work with an artistic director who wants to explore the art form of shadow sign interpretation, you will have a wonderful creative opportunity. When an artistic director is supportive of innovation in sign interpretation, this affects everyone else involved in production and administration; directors and designers are hired with the understanding that this is an integral part of the program. When an artistic director is not interested in sign interpretation, or views it as a necessary evil, you may have a much greater challenge in working with that theatre company.

There is usually an administrative or business manager responsible for keeping the company running smoothly. There may also be a public relations and marketing director. Sometimes there is one administrative person who handles both departments. As an interpreter, you will often be contacted by someone from the public relations department of a theatre. Usually, someone has contacted the theater to inquire about sign interpreted performances. That inquiry would be handled by public relations, hence that department tends to become responsible for locating and hiring interpreters. When a theatre company regularly offers sign interpreted performances, there is generally a person assigned the specific responsibility of coordinating a signed performance program. This might be an access coordinator, dealing with any special needs from the community, or a specific signed performances coordinator, hired on a consulting basis to oversee the program. More than likely, a staff member is assigned the additional duties of coordinating a signed performance schedule.

The box office/subscription staff are often separate from public relations. These folks coordinate all the ticket sales and seating. Sometimes this is a seasonal job. You will probably request your tickets to view the production through the box office. Box office personnel are the folks who actually meet the community. They have to deal with any problems in ticketing and seat selection. You may be asked to provide information to the box office about how to use a TTY, or how to communicate with audience members who are deaf or hard of hearing. In addition, you might be able to help the box office staff designate which seats will provide the best "sight line" for audience members who need to see the signers.

Most theaters have a development director. This person secures funding for the organization through grant writing, fundraising events, and courting corporate sponsors. A theatre which has made a commitment to accessibility to the arts will include information about their program in funding requests. You might be able to provide the development director with some general information about the Deaf community which would assist their grant writing. There may also be specific sources in your community which target their funding to benefit people who are deaf and hard of hearing. That information would be helpful to a development director.

Other administrative staff might include associate artistic directors, education coordinators, company and/or production managers and a technical director. Each theatre varies greatly in staff and structure depending on their mission and funding.

The Production Team
The production team consists of a director, stage manager, design team and actors. These are the people who will actually produce a finished piece for presentation as a theatrical performance. The director provides the vision for the particular play. It is the direc-

tor's concept which will be transformed into a specific stage picture. The same play with two different directors will usually have two different presentations. Each director emphasizes different aspects of the same script to communicate what is meaningful from their perspective. The director selects the cast for the show, and often chooses the designers. The director is responsible for guiding the entire team to achieve their personal artistic vision.

Assisting the director is the stage manager. During rehearsals, this is the person responsible for the artistic administration of the play. That means keeping track of the line cuts, the blocking, scheduling and breaks, as well as coordinating the design schedules. Basically, this is the person who runs the show. The stage manager will call the cues during the show, give the actors their line notes, train and work with production assistants, and keep everyone informed. Once the show has opened, the stage manager takes onthe responsibilities of a director by making sure the show continues to run as conceived and created by the director.

The stage manager is the key person you will deal with as an interpreter. That's because it is the stage manager's job to coordinate every aspect of the production while maintaining a sense of calm and welcome for the company of performers and technicians. Stage managers are problem solvers. They often know more than the administrators about how to incorporate sign language interpreters. When you are working with a touring company, get the name and phone number of the stage manager as soon as possible. Then make contact! This is the person who will have the answers. Often, it is the stage manager who will find the updated version of the script for you or secure seats in the house for you to watch the production. A good stage manager who supports accessibility will make your theater experience a true pleasure. You will be treated as a skilled and knowledgeable professional, as an equal. Respect your stage manager and you will get the same in return!

The design team consists of a costume designer, lighting designer, set designer,prop designer and technical director. There may also be make-up and hair designers, a music director, fight choreographer and acting/vocal/dialect coaches. You may or may not meet these people and their assistants. If you are shadow interpreting, you will need to know these people. In fact, you will probably have to do some educating. Sign interpreter/performers have specific costume, make-up and lighting concerns. *(See Technical Considerations.)* There might also be a signed performances technical consultant and/or sign coach. This person should be fluent in both sign language and English, and also knowledgeable about theatre. The consultant and/or coach will help with translation and provide feedback during your rehearsal process. This is someone who can work with the design team and technical crew to make sure lighting, costuming, hair-style and make up do not interfere with your performance. If you are being fully incorporated into a production, then you should be treated as any other performer in the show. If you are platform interpreting, you may have some access to the designers, but often you are on your own.

Putting together a production is an intense process. There is a specific timeline culminating in performance. Be sure to express your needs early in the process and make appointments as soon as possible. Costume fittings and learning how to do your hair and make-up require time. The more you can learn ahead of time, the less pressured you will be as you approach production. Rehearsals require actors and directors to focus for extended periods of time.

As an interpreter, you need to be respectful of the rehearsal process. Be observant. Find an appropriate time to talk with designers, actors or stage managers. Do not distract from the process. Make sure you know if rehearsals are "open" or "closed". Sometimes a director may choose to have a closed rehearsal while working on particularly sensitive or intimate scenes. It is best to set a rehearsal schedule and discuss it with the stage manager. Some directors will not mind if you show up at any time to observe while others may prefer pre-scheduled times.

If you are hired before rehearsals begin, ask that your name and phone number are listed on the contact sheet. If you are hired later in the process, make sure to give this information to the stage manager so you can be informed of any changes.

Theatre is a fluid, creative process. This means, things change. You need to be willing to adapt to the changes while ensuring your needs are met. Theatre is also a commitment, not just to a time, but to a group of people. If you sign a contract to perform, you should honor that commitment. If for some reason you are unable to perform, give as much advance notice as possible. You will be working very closely with a select group of other professionals for an intense burst of time. This is usually a wonderful experience. If not, it is temporary and you do not have to work for that theatre company again. Most important and well worth repeating, be professional, respectful, and friendly. The theatre world is like the Deaf community, everyone knows everyone.

You may be hired through an agency. In many cities, interpreter referral agencies provide the link between theatres and interpreters. There are also organizations which focus on providing interpreters for theatrical performances. In these instances, a lot of the educating has been done for you in advance. You will work mostly with the agency to receive contracts, scripts, and rehearsal information, never meeting or working with any of the artistic or administrative staff previously discussed. An agency might audition interpreters for theatres. Working through an agency might be a much easier process, but in reality there are very few of these agencies in existence. If you do happen to live in a city which offers these service agencies, and you want to interpret for theatre, contact the agencies to find out if there are special requirements to be selected for theatrical interpreting work.

Whether you are hired by an agency or a theatre, you should provide a resume and a head shot. The resume should list your education and experience, with emphasis on your acting and theatrical interpreting background. A head shot is a close up photograph which usually includes your shoulders and head. This photo may be used in the program distributed at the performances, so be sure it is a good photo, and one which you don't mind sharing with 1,000 to 10,000 people! You should also be sure to include references. If you have worked at other theatres in the same vicinity, provide a name and phone number of someone who can comment on your performance, as well as your professionalism.

ETIQUETTE

The saying goes, "When in Rome, do as the Romans do." The same is true for theatre. There is language and etiquette specific to theatre which any actor must recognize and learn. As a person who already specializes in languages, interpreters should recognize the acceptance which comes with using proper language in the context of the situation. You need to become familiar with theatre terminology as quickly as possible. Then use the appropriate vocabulary. A rehearsal is not called a "practice". Stage managers are not called "coaches" and dressing rooms are not called "restrooms"! By respecting and using the proper words and phrases, communication will be much more clear, lessening the chance of misunderstandings.

As pioneers in a constantly developing field, we often work with theatre professionals who have little or no experience with theatrical interpreting. But these professionals often have a ton of theatre experience. They are a wonderful resource. The trick is figuring out how to encourage acceptance and excitement about theatrical interpreting while meeting our rehearsal needs without sounding like know-it-alls. The keys are common courtesy, a professional attitude, genuine interest, flexibility and respecting the chain of command. You are working in the theatre culture and need to comply with the behaviors of that culture.

Rehearsals
Rehearsals and production are extremely stressful. There is always a time limit. There are only a certain number of hours to rehearse, and once the show is actually being performed, strict time schedules are followed.

Rehearsal schedules are often distributed and discussed at the first rehearsal. When you receive your copy, talk with the stage manager to decide which rehearsals you should attend. If you are platform interpreting, you probably do not want to attend blocking rehearsals, but will want to observe run-throughs.

Be punctual for rehearsals, in fact, arrive a few minutes early to get settled into the space. If you are observing the rehearsal, you need to be in a location where you can see the stage without obstructing anyone's view or path. During the rehearsal, be quiet! If you need to communicate with someone else, wait until there is a break or write notes. You do not want to be a distraction while actors, directors and stage managers are all trying to concentrate and work on creating the performance. Most directors do not mind if you sign because they realize you need to rehearse as well. When you meet with the stage manager to plan your attendance at rehearsals, clearly state when you would like to observe, take notes, audiotape and sign. If you are planning to sign at the rehearsal, sit in a location where you will not be a distraction. Be flexible. If the director asks you to move or to stop signing, do not argue. At the next break time you can speak with the stage manager and resolve any misunderstandings. Rehearsals are often fun, but they can be stressful. When you deal with stressful situations by complying with requests from a director or stage manager, you will gain their respect and keep the lines of communication open.

If you do make a mistake at rehearsal, do not feel the need to give a lengthy explanation about your actions. For example, if you are late, do not hold up the rehearsal any longer with stories of traffic on the freeway or late buses or broken watches. In fact, if you are late for rehearsal, and you are expected on stage during the rehearsal, you should call the stage manager and simply state that you are late and estimate the time you will arrive. When an actor does not arrive on time for a scheduled rehearsal, stage managers worry. They will immediately begin a search by asking other actors your whereabouts and/or begin calling every number you have listed on the contact sheet. Save them the trouble by calling ahead, but don't eat up their time with explanations. All they want to know is that you are all right and on your way to rehearsal. If you arrive late, make sure to find the stage manager or an assistant and let them know you have arrived.

On first arrival to a theater, actors are expected to write their name or initials on a sign-in sheet. Some theatre companies include the name of the interpreters on this sheet. This practice is more likely to happen when the interpreters are more involved in the rehearsal process or will appear on stage. Also, be sure to use the stage door to get into rehearsals or performances at the theater. There may be a security guard and a sign-in sheet at the stage door as well. This is not a substitute for a sign-in sheet posted by a stage manager in the dressing room area.

The stage manager can be your ally. If you have problems with other actors, with designers, with visitors to rehearsals, or with the director, the first person you should talk with is the stage manager. Explain that you are having a problem and need to know the appropriate way to handle the situation. If you are uncertain of procedure or expected behaviors, talk with the stage manager. If they do not know an answer, most likely, they will know who you need to contact.

Performance
Once the show is up and running, there is a certain degree of relief. The rush to open the show and the pressure of opening night with an audience full of reviewers is past. When the inter-preters arrive for the signed performance, the actors are already into a routine. They have their pre-show warm-ups and rituals which help them prepare for the performance. They are trying to achieve a certain mood or feeling before they make their first entrance onto the stage.

It will be a bit disruptive when the speaking actors realize that this is the day of the sign interpreted performance. Even though it is on the performance schedule, and may be posted on a bulletin board near the dressing rooms, reality often does not strike until the actors see the interpreters heading for a dressing room. Most of the time, the actors are very friendly and excited about the performance being signed. They might ask a lot of questions such as the number of people in the audience attending because the show is interpreted, if you are excited or nervous, perhaps even a question about specific signs you are using during the show. Usually the questions are more numerous when you have rehearsed independent of the cast, as is the situation with touring shows. Be positive and friendly when you answer the questions. For example, at intermission you may be asked how the audience is enjoying the performance. Do not respond by saying, "I think they are bored, the guy in the third row is reading." It is better to say something positive. Remember, the actors are in the midst of a performance and you are not the stage manager nor the director. It is not your place to negatively comment on the show, especially during the performance. If you interpret theatre long enough, you will at some time sign for a show which you think is an awful production. That is your opinion and you are welcome to it, just don't spread it around, especially before or during the performance.

In addition, it is important to remember that actors and directors are very sensitive to suggestions about their performance. One rule of etiquette in theatre is to never tell an actor what to do! This means, if you have an idea about how an actor should or could do their job, keep it to yourself. Acting is a personal experience and people can be very offended by even the most well-meaning suggestions. If you think it is of utmost importance that something be said, tell the stage manager.

You may be assigned a dressing room just for the interpreters, or you may be sharing a room with actors. If you are sharing, be respectful of the other actors in the room. This is not a time to talk about other actors and their performance, or technical problems, or that you do not feel prepared for the performance. Before the show is not a time to be unsettled. If you are having problems, perhaps a costume needs a quick repair or you are not feeling well, the person to talk with, in private, is the stage manager. Otherwise, get a feel for the atmosphere in the dressing room. Do the actors prefer to be quiet or converse? Be respectful of the mood in the dressing room as it is a shared space. Actors and stage crew also congregate in an area affecionately known as the green room. This might actually be a room, or it may be an open space near the dressing rooms. It is a community space for relaxing or warm-ups. There is often food available in this area. All etiquette rules apply here as well.

Before the show there will be calls to warn the actors of the time left before performance. In some theaters this happens over a loudspeaker; in others, the stage manager or an assistant goes to each dressing room and announces, "Half hour to places," then returns for subsequent calls. When the stage manager or a production assistant provides information to a performer in person, it is appropriate to acknowledge that you have heard the information. A simple "Thank you" is often enough.

A production from rehearsals through performance is an intense experience in a limited amount of time. The way to enjoy the experience is through common sense, professionalism and common courtesy.

4. Rehearsal Process

As with any performance, a great deal of rehearsal is necessary to provide the best possible sign interpretation. If you have been hired to work on a production before the first rehearsal, you are lucky! Many theatres hire interpreters at the last minute, so it is a luxury in some ways to have four to six weeks of time to prepare for a performance.

When you agree to sign a production for a theater, ask that a rehearsal schedule be sent immediately. If your main source of income is interpreting work, you will need to block off rehearsal time as far in advance as possible. You also need to be realistic about the amount of time you will need to rehearse. A one hour children's production will usually require far less rehearsal time than a three hour piece intended for an adult audience. A play that uses standard American dialog will require less rehearsal time than a production which incorporates many cliches, puns, or even foreign dialects.

THE FIRST REHEARSAL

The best place to begin is the first rehearsal if possible. Often, the first rehearsal includes the production crew as well as the actors and director. This is a great time to meet everyone involved in the production, since names and responsibilities are part of the initial introduction. As a signing performer attending a first rehearsal, you become much more a part of the team. Often, actors are quite excited to know shows will be signed, and this is a wonderful opportunity to answer questions or clarify the role of the interpreters throughout the production process.

Set Designer
It is common with many theatres to have presentations from the set designer, costume designer and director at the first rehearsal. The set designer will usually display a model of the set and discuss the reason for the design. Specific changes in the stage will

be described, often in great detail. Viewing a model of the set will give you a visual reference point from which to begin understanding the picture the director and designers want to present to an audience. It will also give you an opportunity to see and hopefully determine where the interpreters will be placed during the performance. A set with many levels provides much different sightlines than a set with one level. The rake (the angle of the floor) of the stage and the rake of the audience also contribute to choices about the location of the interpreters. But mostly, taking a look at the set, and listening to the concept of the designer will give you a deeper understanding of the production, and that will influence the choices you make as you prepare for the performance.

Costume Designer

As the costume designer discusses the costumes that will be built for the production, sketches of the costumes are often circulated for actors and production crew to view. This is a wonderful opportunity for interpreters to begin thinking about the colors and style used by the costumer, and how that might best be complimented by the signers during the performance. If you are truly fortunate, the costumer will have designs for the signers. This generally should happen if the signers are shadow interpreting. Even if the costumer does not have specific designs for your costume, often he or she is willing to suggest what type of outfit might best enhance the production. Don't be afraid to ask. If they have not thought about it, your query will start them.

Not every first rehearsal includes set and costume design presentations. Sometimes those presentations happen only at production meetings. There are also many situations when sketches of the costumes might not be available. If there is not information provided at the first rehearsal about the set and costumes, then ask for more information from the theater.

Director/Stage Manager

There is usually a talk from the director and stage manager at the first rehearsal. The stage manager will cover the business aspects and technical considerations that need to be discussed. These include rehearsal times, phone contact lists, special events that might be happening during the run of a show, emergency procedures, and whatever else needs to be addressed.

The director's talk is often one of the best opportunities you will have to get an initial understanding of the concept for a production. During this talk, the director might explain the history related to a production, the playwright's motivation for the creation of the work, and the director's perspective on the meaning of the work and how it will be presented for this particular production. Any of this information, and perhaps all of it, will help you understand the work with much greater depth than if you were to make assumptions on your own. It will also make your interpretation easier because it will be a guide as you make choices about which signs to use or how to express certain elements of the play. (The translation chapter goes into more detail about sign choices.) The same play produced by two different directors may present two entirely different perspectives. It is your responsibility to understand the direction specific to the production you're signing to give the truest rendering of that work in that theater. The first rehearsal is a great time to take notes that you can refer to as you continue to work at understanding and presenting the play.

After all the introductions and descriptions of aspects related to the show, there is generally a first read-through of the script. Usually all the initial cuts are shared, either before or during the actual reading of the script. The production crew will often depart before the reading begins, which leaves the actors, stage manager(s) and director to read through the play. The first reading of the script is a good time to hear the different voices of the actors, and to begin connecting them with the parts they will play in the show. Also, if you are platform interpreting in front of and/or below the stage apron, you won't be able to see the actors, so you will need experience recognizing their voices in order to distinguish their characters. Even though the way the lines are read is not the way they will eventually be expressed by the time the show opens, you will be able to get a sense of the flow of the play, especially with the cuts to the script. The director may also stop and discuss certain aspects of the script during the first read through. For example, the playwright's intent, the use of specific vocabulary choices, pronunciation of words, or whatever other information the director decides to emphasize.

Depending on the number of interpreters working on a production, this is also a good opportunity to begin to decide who will sign each character. Certain signing styles may be more compatible with certain characters in a show. A forceful signing style might match a character who speaks decisively. A signing style which uses a smaller space or is lighter in movement might best suit the role of a child or a shy person. You will often portray more than one character, and hence need to be able to modulate your style to express the vocal characteristics of several characters in the same production. It will make your work easier if your signing style is already compatabile with personalities portrayed on the stage. There also may be a physical resemblance between an interpreter and a character which would make it easier to identify which character is being signed by which interpreter.
Another thing you might learn at this initial rehearsal is whether or not there will be any music added to a production. Sometimes, songs are added to a production, whether or not they were included in the script. A good example of this was a production of *Two Gentlemen of Verona*. The director chose to add specific songs to this updated version of Shakespeare's work. As the audience arrived, actors performed in a cabaret style singing songs such as "Paper Moon" while strolling through the audience. In addition, a jazz singer was added to the cast. She sang verses from a variety of modern songs between scenes. The words and order in which the songs were added was listed on a sheet which was not distributed to the actors. Obviously, this is information an interpreter would need as early as possible.

Now, not all first rehearsals provide all this information, and in fact, some directors may choose to have a "closed" first rehearsal, which only the actors, director and stage manager attend. If this is the case, it is worthwhile to talk with the stage manager and/or director to explain why you would like to attend. Often, the

38

stage manager or director may just not have thought about inviting the interpreters. This is yet another time when the interpreter needs to be an educator. Your job is to present the director's and actor's visions of the production, and you need all the information you can get to help you succeed.

OTHER WAYS TO GATHER INFORMATION

If you are not able to attend the first rehearsal, there are other ways to gather some of the information that may have been presented. The director may have written out director's notes for the playbill, and these will give you some of the information shared with the actors. The stage manager may put out memo sheets with updated information about the production. The public relations department should have information they will use for press releases and program notes that you can access. Usually, there are people willing to talk with you about the show and how it will be performed. One of the best resources is the actors themselves, as they can explain the choices they make for the way they will present their characters.

It is also helpful to familiarize yourself with the work by reading scholarly articles about the play. If the play focuses on a very specific event that happened in history, it is well worth the time to research and read up on the topic. A play might be adapted from a novel or short story — if so, read the original work. If the play is biographical, reading about the person portrayed would be very worthwhile.

In general, your rehearsal process should include information-gathering that will be useful to your understanding of the work you will perform. You want to know the show, and be able to discuss the characters, the language, the history and perspective of the work.

OTHER REHEARSALS TO ATTEND

After the first rehearsal, there are specific times that might offer the best benefit for you to attend. Rehearsal times will vary depending on the theater, and whether or not it is an Equity house. Generally, rehearsals will either take place during the day and early evening, Tuesdays through Sundays, or they will be scheduled in the evening, Sunday through Thursday. Non-Equity houses tend to use the latter schedule. As the production draws closer to opening, there are usually weekend days and nights added to a rehearsal schedule.

The rehearsals that are often the most helpful are run-throughs. These are times when the play will be rehearsed in sequence, and can be either complete run-throughs, when the entire show will be rehearsed, or partial run-throughs when several scenes may be presented. Run-throughs are often several weeks into the rehearsal process, so it is wise to attend rehearsal before that time.

Each director is different when it comes to planning a rehearsal process. Some are extremely specific about setting all the blocking early in the process, others work expressly on the language and meaning of the text and leave the blocking until later. You will need to talk with the stage manager to determine which rehearsals prior to run-throughs might be the most helpful to attend. During a rehearsal of one or two scenes, there will be a lot of repetition of lines and often discussion about the way a line will be delivered. The repetition will help you become more familiar with the language and thus refine your translation, and the discussion will provide additional information about the motivation of the characters. It probably would not be helpful to attend a fight rehearsal, unless you will be shadow interpreting and need to figure out when to duck!

TRANSLATION REHEARSALS

Now that you have attended the first read-through, determined which other rehearsals you need to attend, and done some additional reading and research about the show, you need to determine as a team of interpreters how you will work on the translation of the show. It is a good idea to set a rehearsal schedule which specifically focuses on translation. This may be at scene rehearsals, as the actors may be replaying the same scene several times in a row, while stopping to discuss the meaning of the script. A lot of translation work can be accomplished by listening to the words being spoken and then signing as if you were in a real interpreting situation. Sometimes the time pressure of having to sign in the moment, frees our minds to make terrific sign choices. Other times, it is necessary to work with a script and a dictionary! Depending on the length of the performance and the complexity of the language, give yourself ample rehearsal time for translation. Most of the time you will be interpreting a performance with at least one other interpreter, and possibly more. Some translation work can be done independently, but usually most of the translation needs to be done with the other interpreters to negotiate sign choices. In addition, puns, word-play and even basic dialogue between characters are highly inter-dependent and need to be discussed and translated to maintain consistency and communicate meaning. Some lines of a play are signed in unison, especially in musical productions. A great many hours need to be dedicated to translation time, so the earlier those times are decided, the more prepared the inter-preters will be for their performance.

Rehearsal schedules for speaking actors include dates for being "off book". This means having the lines memorized, instead of carrying a script in hand on stage. For signing actors, it is wise to set a translation schedule, and even to establish a date by which you will have the major speeches of a production translated. For a play with modern English and minimal word play, this will be an easy accomplishment. Shows with intensive language (like Shakespeare) should be worked through scene by scene in order to complete the translation. If a translation consultant is avail-able, utilize their skills to help with the most difficult passages or concepts.

BLOCKING A SHOW

If you will be shadow interpreting a production, your rehearsal schedule will be much heavier and more complicated. This is due to the time necessary to block the interpreter/actors into the stage picture. How and when this process is accomplished varies, depending on the approach a theater has chosen. Some theatre companies will block the interpreters when the actors are being blocked into the scenes. Other theatres may have a separate blocking rehearsal scheduled specifically for the signed performances.

Shadow interpreted performances require a lot of hard work and preparation. Integrating the signing and speaking actors as early as possible will present the best possible performance for all audience members. There is not necessarily a best way to accomplish this feat. Every director approaches the rehearsal process in their own preferred style. Many directors have never worked with shadow interpreted performances. It is important to be as flexible as possible when establishing a rehearsal schedule, while making sure the needs of the signing actors are met.

If your blocking is created at the same time as the actors, this gives the signers optimum time to rehearse the blocking and get the movements into muscle memory. Actors become physically used to their stage movements and, after much repetition at numerous rehearsals, their movements and blocking become "automatic" because they have been physically repeated enough to be encoded into muscle memory. Signing performers often have much fewer blocking rehearsals and often arrive on stage worrying about their next blocking move. That is why the earlier the signers are blocked into the show, the better! There is enough to think about while on stage besides where you need to move and when. Suppose there is a six week rehearsal period: during the second week, the director will usually schedule the first blocking rehearsals and will set the blocking for each scene in the show. This process requires a lot of starting and stopping. Therefore, it is a good time to put the signers into the show as well. Granted, blocking often changes once the rehearsals move to the actual set, but getting a head start on the blocking will save a lot of time closer to the opening and reduce the overall stress for everyone in the production. It will also let the actors, both signing and speaking, become used to sharing the space. Directors who are eager to work with signers on stage will create two stage pictures simultaneously: one which includes the signers and one that does not. These directors are rare, but they do exist!

Another opportunity to block the signers into a production occurs if the rehearsals are held at a different location from the actual performance space. When the production moves to the actual set, many directors use the first and sometimes the second rehearsal in the performing space to go through the show scene by scene, adjusting the blocking. Whether or not the signers have already been blocked into some or all of the production, this is an excellent opportunity for checking and/or setting the blocking. Depending on the number of interpreters in the production, it is important to make sure that the signers can get from one location to the next easily without disrupting the look of the production. For example, if the set portrays the interior of a house, with different rooms, a staircase, and perhaps a room or two on the second floor, this will present some logistic problems if there are only two signers for the entire production, and action switches quickly from a first floor location to a second floor location.

Some theatres provide a separate, one-time-only blocking rehearsal for the signed performances. This may be a three- or four-hour rehearsal which requires all the actors to be present, as well as the director or sign designer. During this type of rehearsal, it is best to do what is known as a cue to cue. In this process, the lines that are spoken are only those used to cue the actors' movements. Figuring out when and how the signers will move is the goal of this type of rehearsal. One way to get the most out of this experience is to recruit a volunteer to come to the rehearsal and draw the blocking for the signers as it is decided. This can be expedited by providing photocopied sketches of the stage layout. The volunteer should be someone who is familiar with theatre and organized enough to be able to make notes quickly and accurately, drawing the locations of the signers and noting their entrances, exits, blocking movements within scenes and cue lines. Because a single blocking rehearsal is a relatively brief time to block signers into an entire show, it is often difficult for the signers to clearly notate every blocking move in their scripts. If possible, this rehearsal is also a good time to plan moments when speaking actors can interact with signing actors to make the total performance more integrated.

Another tool useful during the blocking rehearsal is a video camera. If possible, videotape the blocking rehearsal so you can review it if there are questions or concerns about the blocking.

A single blocking rehearsal is better than nothing, but does require someone to run the rehearsal smoothly and efficiently. Someone has to take responsibility for directing the signers and the speaking actors, with the goal of integrating and enhancing the stage picture for the shadow sign interpreted performances. There is also the temptation for actors, fight choreographers and others to try and solve problems that do not relate to the signed performances during this rehearsal time. A director or sign designer will be able to keep everyone on task. However, if the signers will be involved in fight scenes, the fight choreographer must work with the director/sign designer and the signers to incorporate the signers safely into the fight sequences.

Once the signers have been blocked into the production, they will need to rehearse their blocking. Consult with the stage manager to schedule times to walk the set. It is useful to write out your blocking on small index cards. Include your entrance, any cue lines, where you will move, your exit and any other necessary information. Referring to the index cards, walk the set to help get your movements into muscle memory. *(See SAMPLE BLOCKING CARDS in the Appendix.)* The more time you are able to spend on the stage, the more comfortable you will be during the performance, presenting a higher quality production overall. Memorize your blocking to the point that it is automatic. Your walk-throughs on the set should be rehearsed with the other signers in the show.

LIGHTING TECHS

Once the blocking is set, a lighting tech will allow the lighting designer and a deaf technical consultant to set the cues for the signed performances. The lighting tech usually requires two to three hours and should be attended by the lighting designer, sign designer and/or director, signing performers and a technical consultant who is deaf and knowledgeable about theatrical productions. The lighting designer, assisted by the light board operator, should display each light cue in the show in sequence. The signers will demonstrate their blocking (remember those handy index cards?) and the technical consultant will alert the lighting designer to scenes that require light cue adjustments. Believe it or not, lights can be either too dark or too bright! Often, minimal adjustments are required. Sometimes lights might need to be added to a scene or perhaps the light level needs to be adjusted slightly more or less. It may be necessary to slightly change the blocking to resolve lighting issues. It is very important to be respectful of the lighting choices which have been made by the light designer and director; those choices were made to set a very specific mood for the play.

For platform interpreted performances, there is usually one light set for the signers which is brightened or dimmed manually during the production. The light is usually set the day of the performance to ensure the signers hands and faces are visible and shadows minimized. Often, there is a single light aimed directly at the signers. This can cast shadows on the face, especially if you have bangs across your forehead. It is important to check that the light is set wide enough to keep your hands visible in the signing space you will use. Stand under the light and sign to make sure your hands do not slip into shadow.

Be creative in solving lighting problems. In one production, there was a very dramatic ending to the first half of the show. An actor kneeled on the stage in a single pool of light, expressing his love for a woman he was forbidden to meet. The stage picture at this moment was exquisite — a powerful emotional statement for the audience. The idea of bringing up a second light on such a small set, and placing a signer in that additional light, would have drastically changed the experience of that moment for all the audience members, deaf or hearing. Instead, the signers translated the speech simply and elegantly and taught the speaking actor the signs. The actor remained the only person lit on the stage, speaking and signing his lines at the same time. The response from the audience was tremendous. The people who could hear were stunned by the beauty of the sign language, the people who depended on the signs were able to see the actor's face and body language directly, and the actor experienced an incredible, powerful connection to every audience member and to the language being expressed by his voice and his hands. While it was initially a way to solve a lighting problem, it became one of the most poignant, beautiful moments in the performance.

DRESS REHEARSALS

As the play moves closer to opening night, people involved in the production deal with the increased stress of getting everything done well and on time. If you will be platform interpreting, you will be mostly an observer during this time. If you want to sign at a dress rehearsal, that should be established early on. This will give the actors and lighting designer or light board operator a chance to see how the signed performances will look. Even sitting in the audience and signing the show at a dress rehearsal provides a good opportunity to hear the voices of the actors as they sound in the theater space. If you are platform interpreting, most likely the actors will be behind you or off to your side, and depending on the acoustics of the performing space and where you are placed, you may need to make adjustments to be able to hear and to distinguish between the voices of the actors. This is a real challenge if the production is all-male or all-female or has a large cast.

As mentioned earlier one thing that will help your rehearsal process immensely is an audiotape of the performance. This should be recorded as early as possible once the play is being performed from start to finish. Often, a first or second run-through is a good time to make an initial audiotape, keeping in mind that the actors will pick up speed as the production nears opening. There may not be the exact sound effects during a run-through, and you will also pick up the sound of the stage manager giving technical notes such as, "Lights out" or "Scene change." The first dress rehearsal is a time to make an audiotape which will include all the extra sounds of the play. The tape can sometimes be made right off the sound board in the technical booth at the theater. Ask the stage manager about having this done by the sound person, if possible. Sometimes, all the tape decks in the booth are already in use to produce the show, which may mean you must bring your own tape player and record either in the theater or from a monitor in the booth. However it is accomplished, an audiotape will allow you to hear the show and rehearse it away from the theater. You can replay specific parts as often as you need to get your timing synchronized and to help you memorize the order of events in the play.

Most productions have a minimum of two dress rehearsals and two preview performances. Try to sign one of each. This gives all the actors, signing and speaking, opportunities to run through the entire production as an ensemble. It will also give any technical consultants and/or sign designers an opportunity to view the show and make notes for the signers about their acting, translation, visibility and movement. Just as speaking actors receive notes about their performances, signing actors also need feedback to improve their performances. The lighting cues set for the signed performances can also be double-checked during a dress rehearsal and preview performance. The technical consultant should attend both, and if a specialized translation coach has been hired, he or she should also attend these performances and provide feedback to the signing actors.

A signed dress rehearsal is also another good time to videotape. The signers will be able to review their movements on stage and perhaps spot opportunities to improve interaction with other actors on the stage.

After one theatre company tried a variety of rehearsal schedules, one of the actors spoke out and said to the director of a new production, "I am excited about our shadow signed performances, but when it comes to the rehearsal process, do it right! Incorporate the signers into the show as early as possible; don't throw them in at the end of the process when stress is at the highest level and everyone is tired!"

SPECIAL CONSIDERATIONS

Often, interpreters are hired to sign a performance after the production has already opened. This happens especially when the show is enjoying a long run or when a touring production comes to town. In these situations rehearsals happen separately from the cast and crew, and platform interpreting is the style used during the actual performance. It is still important to gather as much information as early as possible. This includes an accurate copy of the script, an audiotape of the performance, any director's notes, information for teachers, and dramaturg notes. You also need to see the show as often as possible and schedule translation time.

Touring productions provide a special challenge as the show may be in town for only a week or two. The good thing about tours is the availability of commercial audiotapes or compact discs, scripts and programs which will be useful for your rehearsal process. Some shows have been made into movies which are available on videotape; however, there are often many changes from the stage production. But if a videotape is all you have to work with, it is better than nothing.

The rehearsal process must meet your needs as a performer, if you are to provide the best possible show for your audience.

5. Translation Process

Whether it's a children's show, musical or Shakespeare, a script needs to be translated into a signed language, like American Sign Language (ASL) or a code, such as Signed English. Most of the time, translations for theatre lean towards Pidgin Signed English (PSE), which combines ASL with English syntactical structure. If you know your audience, then it will be easier to decide whether to translate in ASL, PSE, or Signed English. American Sign Language lends itself beautifully to any production, especially to scripts which include lots of imagery and poetry. It takes more time to translate a script into ASL, and often requires the assistance of a translation consultant or sign language coach. Signed English may take less time to translate but is much more exhausting during performance. Attempting to sign every word as it is spoken or sung is an enormous task, especially when the lines are spoken rapidly. If you are interpreting a children's production and you know the deaf kids in the audience all communicate using Signed English, you would probably choose to use Signed English. You also may be interpreting for students or adults who are hard of hearing and they may need signs to supplement what they are able to hear with assistive listening devices.

The reality is, most of the time your audience will include people who use a variety of different communication modes along the spectrum, from ASL to Signed English to Speechreading. That is why many translations are Pidgin Signed English. This method allows the interpreter to use ASL where it seems more appropriate and Signed English, or at least English word order, at other times. An example of this might be if you are signing a show which includes popular phrases that have become part of our everyday life. You may decide to sign those specific phrases in English word order. You may also decide to sign popular cultural cliches that appear in the production in English word order. It all depends on the language of the script, the composition of your audience and your own fluency and translation skills.

IN THE BEGINNING

How do you actually go about the process of translating? First, you need to be familiar with the script and with the production. A lot of the information you gathered at a first rehearsal will make your job easier, because you will have a deeper understanding of the choices the director made about a production. The first read-through (which often takes place at the first rehearsal) will also help your translation work as you will be able to hear the play in its entirety, gaining a feel for the flow of the text. Throughout the rehearsal process, the director and the actors will continue to develop the characters in the show, giving more depth to their performances and more insight into what motivates each character to make specific choices of action and language in the story.

You may be wondering why it's valuable to listen to the director and actors talk about the characters. Maybe you are thinking that you can read the script yourself and translate it right from the page. You certainly can achieve a translation using that method, but will it be the best possible translation? If you understand the characters as they are being portrayed in a particular production, it will be much easier for you to make sign choices. There are many ways to sign the same idea, but you need to know how your character would express the idea in sign language. The words in a line might be the same for two completely different characters, but the translation will differ. If your character is from a more aristocratic background, your sign choices would be much different than if the character is poor and illiterate. For example, a wealthy character might be represented with more formal, two-handed signs, while a poor character would use more informal one-handed signs. Or a character may be saying "I love you," and the actor chooses to say it through clenched teeth to achieve a particular effect. Simply reading the script may not give you that information. That's why it is essential to understand your characters.

Your best resource is usually the actors themselves. They are usually more than willing to take some time and talk about their character with interpreters. In fact, many actors will be able to help with your translation, whether or not they know any sign language! Some of your best translations may happen in these instances. For example, suppose you have two or three ideas for how you will translate a particular line or section of the script. Show the actor the different sign choices and explain the nuances in meaning of each particular choice. Through discussion with the actors, they will usually be able to tell you, from the translation choices you have presented, which most clearly expresses the character.

If you are not able to talk with the actors directly about their roles and how they are portraying their characters, then you will need to do a lot of research to aid in your translation. It is useful to read the notes provided with a play and also to read commentary on the play and the significance of the characters. You do need to remember, however, that the same character may be portrayed differently in separate productions of a show. The interpretation of the role depends on choices made by the director and actors. In two different productions, a character may say the line "I was embarassed." For one, the appropriate choice may be the standard, two-handed dictionary sign, EMBARASS. For the other, it may be more fitting to sign, RED (spread-up-face).

ASSIGNING CHARACTERS

One of the first tasks of the translation process is deciding which interpreter will sign for which characters. There are a number of ways to decide: gender, signing style, familiarity with a character and even physical resemblance to the actor portraying that role. In most plays, the number of roles requires that interpreters sign for more than one character. Often there are only two or three interpreters signing for a production which includes anywhere from five to forty characters!

The first place to begin is with the central characters of the play. It is a good idea to try and assign a major character to each interpreter and maintain that character throughout the play. If the story revolves around two best friends, then each friend should be signed by a different interpreter. This will help the audience follow the characters throughout the show. Other characters should be assigned by figuring out who plays opposite whom in which scenes. In a play such as *Romeo and Juliet,* one interpreter would sign Romeo and the other Juliet. Romeo's friend, Benvolio, will probably be signed by the same interpreter who signs the role of Juliet, because Benvolio appears opposite Romeo in a number of scenes and never talks with Juliet himself. The interpreter signing Romeo might also sign the role of the Nurse, because the Nurse and Juliet have several scenes with each other. Now it becomes complicated, because the Nurse also has a lengthy scene with Romeo. This is the time when you wish for more interpreters to divide the roles! If there are only two interpreters, then probably the Nurse will be signed by the interpreter who usually signs Juliet, but only in the scenes with Romeo. This may seem confusing, but there is a method to this madness! Because it is very clear that Juliet is not participating in the dialog between Romeo and the Nurse, the audience will figure out who is signing for the Nurse, especially if the same interpreter signs the role of Romeo from the beginning to the end of the production.

Some interpreters may choose to keep the same characters during the show, even though this means one interpreter signing several pages of dialog, while the other interpreter waits for their characters to speak. This can be even more confusing to audience members, especially in a platform interpreting situation where the actors and interpreters may be very far apart from one another. It will sometimes happen that an interpreter will sign for several different characters one right after the other, but usually it is for a minimal amount of time. In those instances, it is important that the attributes of the characters be clearly conveyed by signing style, signing choices and physical expression.

There are other ways to determine who will sign which lines in a show. Sometimes a scene which includes a group of characters will focus on a disagreement between them. There may be three characters who support an idea, and their lines could be signed in succession by the same interpreter.

For example:
> *Character one: "We can't let this happen!"*
> *Character two: "It will change everything!"*
> *Character three: "We won't let you do this!"*

These three lines are spoken by different characters with the same perspective, and hence could be signed very easily by one interpreter, especially if there is a fourth character who has an opposite viewpoint.

Another way to assign characters is to look at what the characters represent. This works best when there are either very few characters in the show or when you have more than two interpreters! If there are only two interpreters and the story is about a war between Germany and the United States, it would be difficult to have each interpreter always represent characters from one country. Suppose the first scene includes only German characters and the next scene has only American characters. It would be confusing to have one interpreter sign all the German characters in one scene, because the audience would have a difficult time following which character is speaking. The German characters would need to be divided between the two interpreters. When scenes include both German and American characters, it might work for one interpreter to sign exclusively for each nationality. However, with more than two interpreters, two interpreters could represent characters from each country. This allows the interaction between the characters to be more clearly represented by the signers. Unfortunately, there are usually only two interpreters hired for a production. In that case, you would divide the characters to recreate the traditional back and forth exchanges which occur in the play.

When shows are shadow interpreted, it is much easier for the audience to see which interpreter is signing for which character. In some scenes however, there may be a large number of actors and only two interpreters. In these instances, the blocking of the interpreters may determine who signs which lines. If one interpreter is near a group of actors on a staircase and another is at the bottom of the stairs, it may work for each interpreter to sign for the actors in their zone. There are a lot of factors to consider when choosing who will sign for which characters, as well as a lot of opportunities for creativity in dividing up the lines of a show.

PREPARING THE SCRIPT

Once you have determined your characters in the show, mark your script. You may do this by highlighting the names of your characters. You may also want to highlight their lines. Then you begin the translation process. The first thing to do is read through the script and find the parts you do not understand. It may be there are specific words you need to look up in the dictionary or historical references you need to understand to translate the script. There may also be words spoken in dialect or a foreign language. Another thing to look for are puns, jokes and cliches. All of these can be a challenge to translate. Place names, proper names and references to famous people should also be marked in your script. You may circle these with a pencil or with alternate marker colors. You will also need to note where specific sounds will occur during the production. There might be a siren, a door slam, a telephone ringing or traffic noises. These all need to be communicated during the production, and if they are not conveniently mentioned in the dialog, or visually obvious on the stage, then you will need to include them in your translation. A great time to do this is at the first read-through. As the actors speak their lines, follow along in the script and circle in pencil the places you realize will need extra attention or additional research. You may choose to note it in the margin of the script. Another technique is to mark it with a pencil and then fold down the top corner of the page or use a paper clip to help you find these trouble spots more quickly. I also use brightly-colored adhesive tape flags. These are small rectangular-shaped pieces of tape, half of which are transparent, and the other half a bold color. They stick easily to the script pages. The color tabs, sticking out from the edge, work as markers to find your place. In addition, you may write on the transparent tape with pencil, and it is erasable. These tapes are re-usable as well. After my first time through the script, marking difficult translation points, there are many of these tapes sticking out along the edges of the pages. As I work through the script and make decisions about translations,

I remove the tapes and store them to use again in the future. Sometimes I choose to use several different colors. I may use hot pink to show places in the script where there is an exchange between characters that requires working with my team interpreter. Then I use blue to mark places where I have to make specific translation choices. *(See SAMPLE OF MARKING THE SCRIPT in the Appendix.)*

Once you have noted these areas, get to work finding out what is meant. You may have footnotes in the script, or you may need to do some additional research. Again, the actors, director, stage manager and publicity manager should be able to provide you with explanations about some of the more obscure information in the script. You will also find a lot of information in commentaries and critiques of the script. Shakespearean works are great because they are often published with information about the work, the historical context of the play and footnotes which explain much of the archaic language and historical references. The Oxford English Dictionary (OED) is also a wonderful resource. It is available at most libraries and lists all the meanings of obscure or archaic words. This is very helpful for Shakespeare or other 17th and 18th century plays. Other works do not provide this information, but you can usually find lots of articles or additional materials which will enable you to understand the play.

When making sign choices, there are some important artistic and practical considerations. The further away from the audience you are situated, the larger you will need to sign. It will be helpful to choose signs that use both hands, as these will be seen more clearly than signs using only one hand. Some signs can be signed with either one or two hands, such as the sign, HAPPY. For theatrical purposes, you would be better off signing with both hands. Another situation is when there are two signs to express the same meaning. IF can be signed either near the forehead, (as in SUPRISE or IDEA) with one hand; or it can be signed with two hands in front of the body, the same way JUDGE or COURT is signed. On the stage, it might be a better choice to use the two-handed version of the sign. This makes the sign bigger, so that it is easier to see from the audience. It also allows audience members to rely more on their peripheral vision to take in the sign and the stage picture. Because it takes a bit longer to produce this sign, the audience has more time to watch the action on the stage, rather than looking only at the signer. This will also help to lessen the eye fatigue experienced by many deaf and hard of hearing people who attend theatre. A sign which requires a larger space and movements is less strain on the eyes than constantly trying to focus on smaller signs which are produced more rapidly. Additionally, the sign IF, produced with two hands, gives the signer a lot more flexibility in the way the sign is expressed. The inflection given to the sign can shade the meaning to match the character's vocal expression.

Sometimes you may decide not to sign specific lines in a script, sort of a selected deletion. If you will be platform interpreting, then you will want to give the audience time to watch specific moments on stage. Perhaps there is a romantic kiss approaching, or a daring leap, or the sudden appearance of a character. In one production, the show focused on a sorcerer and there were many special effects used on stage, such as fireballs being hurled at actors, trap doors through which actors would magically appear or disappear. The show's highly visual theme required the platform interpreters to delete some lines in order for the audience to watch the excitement on stage. Sometimes it will require combining a few lines together and then dropping your hands and facing the stage to cue the audience to look there as well. Other times, it may mean just dropping lines completely. You have to decide what is the more important information: what will be seen on stage or what you will sign. If both are critical to the understanding of the show, then you will need to figure out how to provide the signed information, even if it means editing the script to meet your needs. After all, the audience wants the dialog, but they also came to the theatre for the spectacle, the actors, the set, the action and the special effects.

Be aware of gestural movements that might be made by the actors during the production. Sometimes an actor will choose to use specific gestures at specific moments in the play. Watch for these carefully, and if there is a way to match the movement with a meaningful sign, then this will enhance the overall presentation. It may also be that the actor is using a specific enough gesture that you do not need to sign the lines. Again, you will need to determine if there is enough time for the audience to see the gesture and the interpreter clearly, without becoming confused. If the interpreters stop signing, the audience will tend to look towards the stage, and it must be timed perfectly so the audience does not miss the gesture. Sometimes, actors are eager to incorporate signs into the production at planned moments. This can also enhance the performance.

THE PROCESS

Here's an approach I often use to enhance translations:

1. As mentioned earlier, you must know the play. Gather as much information as you can about the work using strategies described earlier.

2. Divide the characters between interpreters and highlight the script.

3. Go through the script and circle any words, phrases or references you do not understand, and research their meanings.

4. Sign through the script once. Often, my team and I will play with the language while attending rehearsals or will listen to an audiotape of the show and sign "inspirationally". This means signing without rehearsal, while the show is being performed, either live or on tape. Because there is no time to stop and think about the translation in-depth, there are some wonderful on-the-spot translations which occur. While my team is signing, I may make some quick reference notes, or my team may make notes about my translation while I am signing. This is often a great way to begin. In the "interpreting" mode, you are forced to make choices quickly, which gives the translation process a jump-start. This also gives you an opportunity to mark passages, pages or scenes which need extra attention. We may sign through the script several times to become more familiar with the show, before making extensive translation choices. We may also attend rehearsals where one or two scenes are being repeatedly

rehearsed. This is a great opportunity to really work on a scene and become completely familiar with its content.

5. Work through the script — signing, writing and brainstorming. My team and I will establish a separate rehearsal schedule for ourselves. During those sessions we work through the script together making translation choices. We usually begin at the first page and go through the script, signing our translations to each other or sharing ideas. Remember all those paper clips or tape flags we used to mark the script? This is also the time we work through those areas. We may decide to begin our sessions by working through all the difficult areas first. Each team comes to an agreement about where to begin. If there is a limited amount of time to prepare for a production (as is often the case with touring productions) we will probably focus on difficult passages first, rather than working through the script page by page. We will also work on songs which require both of us to sign at the same time. When there is a time crunch, it is more important to make sure you and your team know how you will sign things that require agreement. For example, in the *Rocky Horror Picture Show*, the phrase "time warp" is used by several characters in one of the songs. Since both interpreters were signing different parts of the song (an ensemble piece), we needed to agree on how we would sign that phrase. How did we agree on what to sign? We brainstormed. That means, we both came up with as many different ways as possible to sign that phrase, and then selected which one worked the best in terms of clarity, fluid signing movements and rhythm. In addition, we worked with a sign coach, presenting our translation ideas and incorporating his feedback. In the end, we decided on a translation which not only conveyed the meaning of the phrase, but allowed us to shadow the gestures used by actors in their dance.

Continuity of Sign Choices
As you are working through the script, check for continuity of sign choices. This means you and your team are using the same signs for words or phrases that are repeated throughout the play. For example, in *Phantom of the Opera* my team and I developed a name sign for the Phantom which we both used consistently throughout the production. However, characters in the show also

refer to a phantom, meaning a ghost. As a team, we worked together to clarify when we would be signing the name sign or the sign, GHOST.

There are times when you will choose different signs to represent the same English word. This is most often the case with comedies which rely on word play and punning to create humor. Deciding how to convey a pun is quite a challenge. A pun creates humor by using the same word to convey different meanings. In sign language, a similar effect may be acheived by using the same hand shapes to convey different meanings as well. For example, in Shakespeare's *The Taming of the Shrew.*

> *Widow.* Thus I conceive by him.
> *Petruchio.* Conceives by me! How like Hortensio that?
> *Hortensio.* My widow says, thus she conceives her tale.
>
> (V.ii)

In the Widow's line, the word conceive means, "to understand." The interpreter used the sign, UNDERSTAND. Petruchio uses the word conceive to create a pun, questioning if he has impregnated the Widow. The interpreter used a combination of two signs: UNDERSTAND (signed in front of the belly, popping up from below, to project through the fingers of the other hand) and PREGNANT (signed with both hands moving forward to represent an expanding belly). Hortensio's use of the word conceive means the Widow finally got the point. The interpreter signed UNDERSTAND as it was signed for Petruchio's line, but placed the sign at the forehead rather than the belly, as if something were piercing her forehead. The same hand shapes were used repeatedly to emphasize the repetition of the word conceive. As this example illustrates, it is important to work together as a team to achieve a translation which best represents the meaning of the language, especially when the same word is used to convey totally different concepts.

Name Signs

You and your team will need to develop name signs for characters and places referred to in the play. This is a very subjective process. Here are some guidelines to make the process easier. First, decide which characters and places absolutely require name signs. You will find that there are many characters who do not need name signs. Perhaps their costumes or actions on stage make it clear who they are, such as a waitress or pilot. Characters in minor roles may not need name signs. Sometimes a messenger runs on stage for one or two lines, and a name sign might only confuse the audience. Remember, audience members are working hard to understand the play and figure out who is signing for each character. Adding too many name signs can overwhelm the audience and make it difficult for them to follow the show.

Once you have determined which characters require name signs, take a look at those characters. Sometimes you will want to develop name signs based on physical characteristics, costumes or make-up. An imposing bearded character might be best recognized by a boldly performed sign indicating the beard. Choosing name signs for characters should be very much like choosing name signs for people in everyday life. You may want to locate all the signs for one family in a certain location such as near the heart or forehead.

Whatever name signs you create, make certain you convey this information to the audience clearly each time a new character enters the stage. This may be done by pointing to the character and showing the name sign at that time. You may also want to prepare a name sign information sheet for the audience members. This would be distributed before the play or may be incorporated into the program. *(See NAME SIGN AND INFORMATION SHEET in the Appendix.)* Another option is to offer a pre-show demonstration during which you meet with audience members and review the name signs you will use throughout the production. You will also be able to explain other translation and performance choices, such as how you will cue the audience to look at the stage.

It is especially tricky when people are referred to in a script but are never actually seen on stage. Recurring references to relatives, friends, or places may require a name sign. If you are able to substitute words such as SISTER or CHURCH in lieu of a proper name, it is often best to do so. Once again, informing the audience ahead of time through printed matter or a pre-show demonstration will help lessen confusion. Choosing name signs does not have to be a difficult process; in fact, it is often a great deal of fun.

Fingerspelling

The best advice I can offer is to fingerspell as little as possible. If you do not have to fingerspell, don't. To try and read fingerspelling from the audience under theatrical lighting conditions, and often from far away, is almost impossible. In addition, it requires the undivided attention of the audience member, pulling their focus away from the action on stage. Many interpreters are tempted to fingerspell when there are references made to famous people or events in history for which there is no established sign. This is a wonderful opportunity for you to be very creative and figure out how to represent that information without fingerspelling.

There may be some instances where you choose to fingerspell, usually to convey a specific word or name that is integral to the understanding of the play, or if a character is actually spelling a word. The key thing to remember is "Less is more."

6. Watch rehearsals and/or performances before your own performance. This is a great time to see the props, costumes, make-up and blocking of the finished work. These are all factors which affect your translation. You may decide to make translation changes, including name signs, depending on what you observe. You also need to become familiar with the sounds of the actors' voices in the theatrical space. If you have been working with an audiotape, you will notice a substantial difference in the way voices sound. In many instances, you will be platform interpreting, which means the voices will be behind you, and often you will not be able to see the characters while they are speaking. You need to know where they are placed on stage and who is talking. You also need to observe their actions on stage and make translation changes to reflect or echo their movements. Productions will incorporate new changes through opening night performances. Lines will be deleted or added; the way a line is delivered might change substantially, requiring a complete change in part of your translation. Something that was once serious may now be

a comic line, and your translation will need to reflect that.

7. Some additional suggestions:
- Don't lose jokes. The entire audience should laugh at the same time.
- Don't invent jokes. The audience watching you should not be laughing while others are crying.
- Don't steal focus. The play's the thing. You are there to enhance the performance. The whole audience should not be watching you, and your performance should allow the audience to watch the actors as much as possible.
- Don't invent new signs; it will only confuse everyone.
- Less is more. Keep your translation brilliant, inclusive and brief. This means once you have translated, continue to edit. Initial translations tend to be overtranslated. Also, you should finish signing by the time your character finishes talking.
- Don't over-explain things. Give the deaf audience a chance to figure out things that the hearing audience is allowed to figure out.
- Don't translate foreign languages unless specific phrases, universally understood, are used. For example, don't translate someone spouting Greek if no one is expected to understand it. Do interpret words such as *bonjour* or *ciao*.
- Ask for feedback from people you trust. This will help improve your skills.
- Realize there are many choices that could be made for any theatrical work. You will develop your own personal style over time.
- Have fun.

It is difficult to describe actual translation of plays into signed language using a written form such as this book. Hopefully, this chapter will provide some insights into the process of translation. As you gain experience and confidence, you will develop a process which works best for you as a theatrical interpreter.

6. Technical Considerations

A performance is an integration of many effects which include lighting, costuming, and make-up. As a performer, you are presenting a mask of sorts to the audience. You are taking on the role of another and leaving yourself behind. This is achieved through language, expression, physicality and technical effects.

COSTUMES

As a signing performer, your hands and face are your means for communicating the performance to the audience. They need to be seen. To be seen, there needs to be contrast between the color of your hands and the background — your clothing, your costume. For many years, interpreters have worn black while interpreting for theatre. The theory was a black background would provide optimal contrast for Caucasian signers. A dull black, like cotton, does not reflect light, making it seem even more suitable for a theatrical situation. From the theatre's perspective, the signers were not part of the show, hence black (a neutral color) was appropriate. Production assistants responsible for moving scenery and props between scenes are traditionally dressed in black, so it seemed logical to dress the other technical people in black (signers, of course, being considered a technical rather than artistic aspect of the performance).

Many people still do wear black for theatre, whether platform or shadow interpreting. This is not a necessity. Theatre lights are "hot" lights. They tend to be much brighter than lights we use everyday in homes or businesses. This can exaggerate the contrast between the hands and background, creating greater eye fatigue for the audience. In addition, it is not necessary for seeing the signs. If you have attended theatre performances by actors who are deaf, such as the National Theatre of the Deaf, you will notice they have not worn only black clothing. Many of the technical consultants who are deaf are encouraging interpreters to wear colors other than black for performances.

Colors that work well are purple, darker shades of blue, green, maroon, brown, dark grey, dark reds and jewel tones. You want to avoid colors similar to your skin tone, as your hands will tend to "disappear" under the lights.

You also want to avoid material that is exceptionally shiny or reflective, otherwise you will create a situation with too much glare. The audience will be forced to squint to see your hands!

How do you go about selecting what to wear? If you are shadow interpreting, you need to work with the costume designer and director to create a costume. The director will need to collaborate with the signers and/or a consultant to establish the characters you will portray in the show. Will you be costumed as servants, soldiers, fairies, or courtiers? Once your role has been established, the costume designer will create the initial concept. As a shadow interpreter, you will be moving a lot and, therefore, need to be comfortable. Often, there are only two interpreters in a production, which means you could be on stage for the entire production. You do not want to be uncomfortable. Will you be standing the entire time? Or will you be climbing stairs, sitting on a chair or on the stage? Will you be running or jumping or dancing? Make sure you know how much movement is required before you are costumed. You need to be able to move your arms freely, but you do not want a costume with excessively bulky sleeves. You also may not want a costume that is too low cut, otherwise you lose part of the contrasting background for your hands. Do you need soft-soled shoes if you will be moving during quiet scenes or walking up and down noisy stairs? These are all factors you need to be thinking about.

Costume designers and builders are often not familiar with the needs of signers. Once you have talked about your character, the basic needs for movement and contrasting background, you also want to look at the patterns of the fabric. As a general rule, avoid stripes and dots! But other patterns might work well. A dark color with a pattern of small flowers might be fine. Several dark colors swirled together into a paisley might also be appropriate. Your goal is to enhance the look of the production. You need to look like you are part of the cast, because you are! The more inte-grated you are in terms of placement, movement and costume, the less you will stand out as "The Interpreter." The last thing you want to be wearing on stage is a smock! The audience members watching your signs will appreciate the fact that you are costumed in the same style as the cast.

Another important consideration for costuming is the assign-ment of roles. If you are signing the role of a character who wears a lot of blue, you would want to wear something with similar colors. This will help the audience identify your main character. One way to approach this is to design a costume which includes swatches of the same fabric or color as the lead character you will sign. There are many creative approaches to explore. You also want to retain a sense of the same style. A show set in the Jazz Age should reflect the style of the period. If you are choosing your own costumes from your wardrobe, look for colors that compliment your characters. Sometimes a show will be designed such that conflicting characters will wear conflicting tones. Perhaps one group wears mostly purples and greens while anoth-er wears reds and yellows. You would want to choose colors that fit the design, and still allow you to maintain adequate contrast. If you are a female and will be signing a male character, wearing pants instead of a skirt will also help the audience identify your character.

A signed performances consultant can work with the interpreters and the costume designer to maximize the practical needs of the interpreters and their audience while maintaining the integrity of the production.

HAIR AND MAKE-UP

One of the most important features used during signing is your face. The characters and the emotions they experience will be expressed through your facial expression. Facial features can be enhanced through the appropriate use of make up, but first and foremost, make sure your hair is not covering your face! You may look in the mirror at home and think that your hair does not in any way obscure your face, but under a glaring stage light suspended high above you during a performance, your hair may cast shadows that darken your face, making it difficult for the audience to read your expressions and understand the play. Your hairstyle should complement the style of the production. If you are a woman and have long hair, and the female characters in the show wear their hair in a bun, you might choose to do the same. Likewise, if their hair is worn down, you could wear yours in a similar style, making sure that it is away from your face as needed. Men should be aware of the styles of the male characters. Perhaps their hair is slicked back or styled to match a specific time period. In many cases it will enhance the overall performance if the signers match or complement the hairstyles portrayed on stage. If outrageous wigs are used in the show, or if you prefer not to style your hair like the speaking performers, then a simple, understated hair style is the best choice. Whatever you decide, your hair should not be a distraction to you or the audience. Make sure your bangs are short enough to allow your eyebrows to be seen clearly. Long bangs also create distracting shadows under stage lights. Be sure that you have someone specifically check for shadows while you are under the lights. You will also need to remember to keep your chin up. Looking down while signing from a platform placement will remove your face from the light and the audience will not be able to see your expressions.

Make-up greatly enhances the ability of the audience to see your facial expressions during performance. Stage lights, especially the white lights used for platform interpreting, tend to bleach the color out of any skin tone. Proper use of make-up will help the audience see your face, lessen glare reflecting from your skin and accentuate the facial characteristics you need to communicate your characters.

You may have a skin tone that looks great under the lights without the use of any foundation, but if you are someone who needs to use a foundation, make sure that it matches your skin tone; otherwise, your skin will appear as a different color under the lights. For example, using a foundation for pink skin tones when your skin is olive tone might be fine during regular daily usage, but under the glare of stage lights, your skin may appear orange! Once again, it is a good idea to have someone check your make-up under the actual performance lighting situations. If you are shadow interpreting a performance, you may have the benefit of a consultation with a make-up designer, who will prepare a make-up chart for your use. This designer will also be responsible for checking your appearance while on stage at some point in the rehearsal process.

If you do not have the benefit of a make-up designer, and particularly if you have never consulted with anyone before about your make-up, you might want to invest in a visit with a professional theatrical make-up designer. These folks can teach you a great deal even in one hour and often charge reasonable rates. In the meantime, here are some general considerations:

If you have light eyebrows, darken them with an eye shadow or eyeliner color that matches the color of your eyebrows. Depending on the show and the effect you want to create, you might want to use a darker color on eyebrows of a lighter shade, but generally, you are seeking to emphasize the eyebrows. Remember, under stage lights, your features tend to get a bit "washed out" and need to be highlighted.

If you have very dark, long eyelashes, you might not need to use mascara, but as a general rule, it is a good idea. (To be honest, a lot of men never use mascara for stage, but it is worth experimentation until you find out what works best for your face.)

You always want to use an eyeliner to accentuate the shape of your eyes. (As Stanislavsky said, "The eyes are the windows to the soul.") Either use a pencil with a darker shade such as black, brown or deep purple, or use a dark powder and apply with a fine edged brush. The powder tends to give a softer overall appearance to the eye. It will depend on the style of the production, and what effect you are trying to create. Browns give a more natural look, while blacks create a particular style of character.

colors of the show. Observe the make-up of the actors in the cast and this will give you an idea of the effect being created by the designer. As an interpreter, you need to consider your proximity to the audience. If you are on a platform directly in front of your audience — hopefully you are not — your make-up does not need to be as exaggerated as the actors'. Actors on a proscenium stage are usually separated from the audience by a fair distance and hence their make-up is bold in color, location and shaping to compensate for features that tend to disappear with distance and theatrical lighting.

Use a lipliner to highlight the shape of your lips, and choose a lipstick color which compliments your skin tone, costume and the style of the show.

If you have especially light colored skin, or if you use any base, you may need to accentuate your cheekbones with a powder blush. Once you have completed your make-up, (even if you are not using any base or blush) you should apply a light powder to reduce the shine on your face.

Whatever your make-up choices, be sure to have someone look at your make-up under performance conditions at least several days before the show. If you will be attending a session when the lights will be focused for your performance, that is a perfect opportunity to wear your stage make-up and have someone view you from the audience under your performance lights, taking specific notes on your make-up. Is it overdone? Not enough?

Professional theatrical make-up designers can be located through the theatres where you are performing. Often there are shops which specialize in make-up for theatre and you should be able to get advice and/or referrals. There are also books written exclusively on the topic of theatrical make-up techniques which include illustrations and photographs.

A few other tips. Look out for tan lines! These might be from watchbands, bracelets or rings. Or maybe you wore a three-quarter length sleeve outdoors but in a show you are wearing short sleeves. Make sure the skin is an even tone by applying foundation where needed.

If you are wearing a costume with a low neck line such as a v-neck or a scoop neck, you might need to apply foundation to your skin, especially if your skin is very white in appearance. The glare from stage lights, and your hands signing in front of a white background, often make it difficult for your signs to be seen clearly. The key is to provide contrast so that your hands are easily seen from seats close up and further back in the audience.

LIGHTING

Platform interpreters are often lit by one light focused in a straight line at the performing space. This light is usually at a 45 to 60 degree angle, is often white light, and is usually focused on the day of the signed performance, an hour or so before the curtain. Ask your stage manager for information on when the light will be focused for your performance. The light usually has "barn doors," which are flaps that allow the lighting technician to widen or narrow the amount of light on the performers.

A typical light focusing session begins by determining exactly where the platform for the interpreters will be placed. Once that is set, the interpreters will stand on the platform and the light will be focused on their location. The interpreters need to move their hands to show the amount of space that will be used for signing. This means putting your hands out to both sides, as well as the lowest and highest points where your hands will move. The lighting technician will adjust the angle of the light and the barn doors to make a "signing space". This is the area which will be lit during the show, and often is a square area from mid-thigh to 6 inches above the head, nearly a full arms length to each side. The lighting technician and the stage manager will work together to ensure there is not any "spill" on the stage. This means the light set for the interpreters will not also light an area on the stage which should be dark.

Many times, the lighting technician is uncertain how much area needs to be illuminated. This means if a light has been pre-set for the signers, it may light the full body length of the interpreters. Usually, that is too large an area to be lit, and stage managers are often relieved to discover a smaller space is more than adequate.

While straight-ahead lighting is the norm, you may work in a situation where you are placed on the stage to one side of, but close to the action. If you are able to work with a lighting designer in advance, it is best to be lit from one light on both sides of the interpreting space. This is true even with platform interpreting below a stage, if lights are available. The lights cross over and eliminate shadows. It is also better lighting for manuveuring, as you will turn to look at action on stage, or step to one side or another to shift your weight.

At all times, you want to make sure that you stay in your light. This means there is adequate light on your face, hands and body as you sign. You will know if you are in the light because your face will feel the warmth of the light. Additionally, watch your hands as you are signing and see if they are in shadow or light. If you use a sign where your hands move to the side (such as GOAL or SUCCEED) and your hand moves into shadow, you have probably taken a step too far to one side and moved yourself out of the light. You also need to be careful about moving backward and forward in your signing space. Perhaps there is a stage behind you and one hour into the show your body is fatigued from standing in one place. You might be tempted to step back and lean your back against the stage. However, if the light was set forward of the stage, you will disappear into shadow. It is a good idea to ask the stage manager to mark the area where you need to stand with a piece of glow tape.

While most lights used for platform interpreting are white, you may have the opportunity to work with a lighting designer or technician in advance and talk about the use of gels. Gels are basically transparent sheets of thin plastic placed over a light to produce a color on stage. You've probably seen productions where there are bright colors illuminating the stage — blues, purples, reds, oranges. This effect is produced with the use of gels.

As an interpreter working under the lights, certain colors will enhance the visibility of your hands and face and soften the glare of lighting. Colored gels will also enhance your make-up. For example, a rose colored gel removes pallor. Soft colors such as lavendar and rose tend to be better than blues and whites, but amber, which may seem to be a soft color, might produce a jaundiced look. The best way to know what works is to try it and see what happens.

Most of the time, the person operating the light board during a performance will bring the light for the interpreters up (on) or down (off) to match the stage lighting and maintain as much of the original lighting design of the show. Often lights will go down during set changes and at the end of each act. It is a good idea to check with the stage manager before the performance and find out how the lights are run for the interpreters. It feels very awkward to have a hot spotlight on you while the stage is dark and there is nothing to interpret! The whole audience stares at you! It is also a nice break to get the heat of the lights off your face and be able to relax in the dark for a moment.

It is also important to figure out if there are times when the stage is dark but the interpreters need to be lit. There might be a scene which happens in the dark or music specific to the plot which needs to be signed. Likewise there might also be moments when the lights do not need to be on the interpreters even though there is lighting on stage. Long action sequences or dance segments are a good example. During your rehearsal process take notes on the lighting which you can share with the stage manager if needed.

SOUND

Depending on where you are placed during a performance, the level of sound is a major consideration. You might be located near the orchestra pit. When signing for musicals, interpreters are often placed in front of the orchestra pit. If the kettledrums are on the same side as the interpreters, it is very difficult to hear the actors' voices during some of the songs. It is also very loud! Some shows have huge speakers placed on the stage pointing straight out at the audience. If interpreters are placed in front of the speakers, there are several considerations. Again, how loud is the sound from the speakers? Some shows blast the sound out to the audience and interpreters benefit from wearing earplugs. This might seem strange, but the sound is so loud that the earplugs do not prevent one from hearing, they just serve to lower the sound level. Also, being directly in front of a speaker, yet close to the stage, might cause a sound delay. First you would hear the voice on the stage and next the voice as it comes through the speaker. When you are working with professional theatres and touring companies, the sound systems are of such high caliber that often there is no delay, but it can happen.

You may be placed in an area known as a "dead space". This means the sound does not carry fully to the area. You might be standing in front of the stage and a bit to one side, yet be unable to hear the actors' voices clearly. This usually happens in shows where the actors are not using microphones, and there is not a speaker system in use. As you stand there, trying to interpret, you feel as if the sound drops in front of you, just out of reach. It is hard to interpret when you cannot hear the actors clearly, so check for these "dead spaces" before you make a decision about the placement of the interpreters.

Sometimes, interpreters have tried to use FM systems to help overcome the problem of a "dead space". This can create another problem which is hearing the show twice. The delay in running the sound through the FM system means you will hear an actor's voice on stage and then after a very brief delay, the voice will be heard through the FM system. One way to make sure you are able to hear is to request that a small monitor be placed in front of you or to the side. A monitor is a speaker which plays the sound directly as it is spoken. You have probably seen these used at concerts. They are set on the stage in front of the band with the speaker pointing towards the band. This allows the band members to hear each other. (If you want to interpret concerts, you will definitely need a monitor to be able to hear the words.)

PLATFORM INTERPRETING

Here are a few considerations for platform interpreting. Be sure you are located in a place where you are not in danger. There should be no pit behind you to step back and fall into, neither should you be crowded into a corner and crammed next to a wall. You need to have enough space to perform and move comfortably. The platform should be large enough to allow a shift in position. You will get tired if you are standing a long time, and when you move slightly, you should not feel as if you will tumble off the side of the platform.

If a show is very lengthy, you might want to consider using a stool, sitting on the edge of the stage or being able to lean against a wall if necessary. If you stand in the same place for a long time, there is a good chance your feet or legs will actually go to sleep! If you choose to stand, but have an opportunity to sit for a few minutes, go ahead and sit. For example, you are signing a musical and there is a long dance section. If there is a place to sit in the front row, or a chair to the side, you may want to give your body a break. It will help you survive during a show where one act may run as long as ninety minutes. You may also want to have a water bottle handy if you have a place to sit and relax for a minute. It gets hot under the lights!

Check to see the type of background behind the platform. If it is a color which blends with your skin tone, you may want to wear a long-sleeved top in a color which contrasts with the background. This will avoid the illusion that your hands are invisible, because they are disappearing into the background. Or see if there is a way to drape the background, especially if there is a distracting psychedelic design behind you.

It may seem there are an overwhelming number of technical considerations, but in many cases, you will be working with technical crews so skilled in their work that your preparation will be a breeze. This is especially true with touring productions which offer signed performances in every city. The stage managers are professionals and they know how to get the job done. You tell them what you need, and they will do whatever they can to help.

Conclusion

So here it is.

The very basic tool to use before you step into the spotlight. This book may seem overwhelming or it may seem incomplete. It feels both those ways to me. There is so much information to impart and more than could be written in a beginning text. But what you hold in your hands is much more than has ever been written. For many of us who have interpreted theatre for many years, there have been no guides, no resources, no text with which to take the first steps through the fourth wall. Sometimes we tripped, and so will you, but maybe not as hard. Much just has to be learned along the way.

But this book is something to hold onto, to refer to, something to help you answer some of the questions you may not know you needed to ask. Over time, as you watch and participate in the experience of interpreting for theatre, you will develop your own paths for each new theatrical journey.

Enjoy the journey.

Appendices

APPENDIX 1
SUPPLY & EQUIPMENT LIST
FOR INTERPRETERS

❏ A pencil with a sharp point and a good eraser (clip-on is optional)
❏ Colored pens/pencils
❏ An assortment of highlighter pens in varying colors
❏ Unlined index cards for blocking notes
❏ A notebook
❏ Three ring binder preferably with side pockets for script and for storing additional papers distributed at rehearsals (Width of the binder depends on the script)
❏ A water bottle
❏ Snacks for long rehearsals and for replenishing blood sugar at intermissions
❏ Coins for vending machines, pay phones and parking meters
❏ A small flashlight (a pen light will do)
❏ A small, portable audiocassette player and recorder with a good microphone
❏ A dual cassette deck for dubbing tapes
❏ An audio cassette deck in your car for listening to tapes of shows
❏ A video camera if appropriate, for recording rehearsals and translation work
❏ A VHS player and TV to watch videotapes
❏ Good stage make up
❏ A kit or bag to carry your stage make up
❏ Facial tissues, cotton swabs, mints, lip balm and small sewing scissors)
❏ A resume, bio and head shot on file and ready to send out for auditions
❏ A good dictionary and thesaurus, preferably portable
❏ A folder with side pockets (if your three ring binder does not have any)
❏ A bag large enough to transport all the stuff you need to bring to rehearsals and performances

APPENDIX 2
CHECKLIST FOR INITIAL CONTACT

Name of Theater_____ Phone #_____

Contact Person_____ Title_____

Show_____ Location_____

Dates of run_____ Type of Performance_____

Signed Performance Dates_____ Times_____

Length of Show_____ Number of character_____

Description of plot_____

Foreign Language/Dialect_____ Music_____

Number of Interpreters_____ Placement_____

Dates to view show_____ Scripts_____

Fee_____ Payment_____ Comps_____

Contract_____ Rehearsal Schedule_____

Director_____ First Rehearsal_____

Stage Manager_____ Phone_____

Pre-show_____ Post-show discussion_____

Costume Designer_____ Phone_____

Translation Coach_____ Phone_____

Lighting Designer_____ Phone_____

Theater Address_____

_____ FAX_____

Additional Notes:_____

_____

_____

Brink Theatre Company

August 30, 1995

1111 SW Miller Blvd.
Anytown, U.S.A.

Letter of Agreement

This is an agreement between Brink Theatre Company and Julie Gebron under the following terms and conditions:

Position:	Signed performance interpreter for SIGN THE SPEECH
Term of Agreement:	Thursday, October 9, 1995, 12 p.m. and Friday, October 10, 1995, 8 p.m. performances. Center for the Performing Arts.
Responsibilities:	Rehearsal and signed interpretation of performances.
Renumeration:	$$$$$ paid within thirty days of final signed performance.
Benefits:	Two complimentary tickets for use at any performance. Other benefits as outlined in the Company Handbook.
Publicity:	The contractor agrees to the use of his/her name and services performed for public relations activities by BTC.
Conflicts:	Listed below are all commitments which may be in conflict with responsibilities to BCT.
Travel Reimbursement:	N/A
Termination:	This agreement may be terminated by either party giving the other two weeks notice in writing.

_____
Executive Producer
Brink Theatre Company

_____
Date

_____
Contractor Signature

_____
Address

_____
Phone

_____
SS#

_____
Date

ALL'S WELL THAT ENDS WELL
William Shakespeare

Bertram

The Count
of Rossillion.

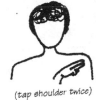

Helena

In love with
Bertram.

(tap shoulder twice)

Count

Rinaldo

A steward in
the household
of Rossillion.

(tap twice)

Captain
Parrolles

(sign twice)

Diana

An Italian woman...
Bertram flirts
with her.

(tap shoulder twice)

Rossillion

• These are the only characters
with name signs.

• Throughout the performance:
Lisa Plymale will sign: King, Parolles
Julie Gebron will sign: Countess,
Bertram

• Other characters will be shared.

APPENDIX 5
SAMPLE BLOCKING CARDS
& NOTES

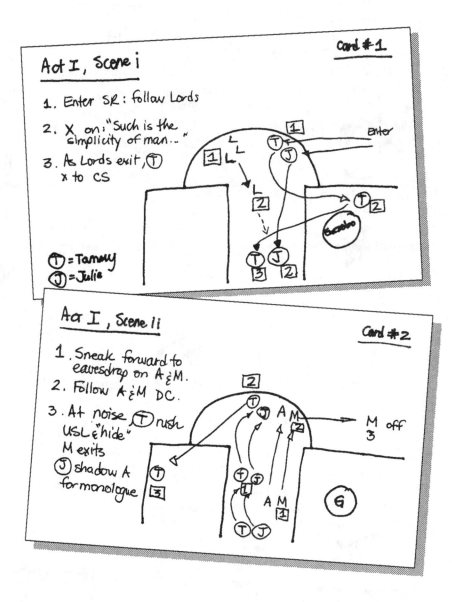

Sample Blocking Cards Notes

Your blocking notes for shadow signed performances will usually be written in the script margins during rehearsals. I find it useful to transfer this information to cards once the blocking is fairly certain. I often do not have the same number of on stage rehearsals as the speaking actors, and like to rehearse my blocking movements when the stage is available. The cards make the rehearsal process much easier. Here are some ideas to help you organize your blocking notes on cards.

- Plain white index cards are great for writing your blocking notes.

- Include a basic stage diagram. It is useful to draw the stage from your perspective as an actor.

- Include location of chairs, tables and other fixed set pieces.

- Decide on symbols to represent the location of signers and characters.

- Make notes about cue lines, entrances, exits and fast or sudden movements.

- Initially, write your blocking notes in pencil. There may be last minute changes. If you know the blocking will not change, you may want to use colored pencils or fine line pens.

- Use a variety of colors to help identify stage movement. Highlighters serve this purpose well.

- Use abbreviations for stage directions *(see Glossary)* to describe your blocking moves.

- Design blocking cards which work for you!

APPENDIX 5
SAMPLE OF MARKING THE SCRIPT

The following script pages from a production of *A Midsummer Night's Dream* show various notations I use to help with the translation process. The translation itself is often written on a blank facing page. On these sample script pages, notes have been written in the margins. Usually, the notes are written on tape flags.

56   A Midsummers Night's Dream   III

Play on words.
Needs to be
play on signs.

Bot.   *Thisbe the flowers of* odious *avours sweet —*
Quin.   'Odorous' Odorous!'
Bot.   Odorous *avours sweet;*

Very melodramatic voice.

      So hath they breath, my dearest Thisbe dear.
      But hark, a voice! Stay thou but here awhile,
      And by and by I will to thee appear.   80

These lines are paired to create meaning.

                   Exit.   [Exit.]

Puck.   *A stranger Pyramus than e'er played here!*
Flu.   Must I speak now?
Quin.   Ay, marry, must you; for you must understand   85
      he goes but to see a noise that he heard, and is to
      come again.
Flu.   *Most radiant Pyramus, most lily-white of hue,*
      Of colour like the red rose on triumphant briar,

Spoken in high-pitched voice.

      Most briskly juvenal, and eke most lovely Jew,   90
      As true as truest horse that yet would never tire;
      I'll meet thee, Pyramus, at Ninny's tomb

Ninny is a silly word – may cause laughter. Need silly sign re: Ninny/Ninu

Quin.   Ninus' tomb man! Why, you must not speak that
      yet; that you answer Pyramus. You speak all
      your part at once, cues and all.   95
      Pyramus, enter! Your cue is past; it ie never tire

Cue line fo entrance – must be signed sar way in all 3 lines.

Flu.   *O — As true as truest horse that yet would* never tire.

Audience must be cued in time to watch this ⟶ entrance – big reaction.   [Enter Puck and Bottom with the ass-head on.]

Bot.   *If I were fair, Thisbe, I were only thine.*
Quin.   O monstrous! O strange! We are haunted! Pray,
      masters! Fly, masters! Help!   100.

      [Exeunt Quince, Snug, Flute, Snout Starveling.]

Hel.   Fine, i faith!
Have you no modesty, no maiden shame,
No touch of bashfulness? What, will you tear
Impatient answers from my gentle tongue?
Fie, fie, you counterfeit! You puppet you!

Her.   Puppet? Why, so? Ay, that way goes the game!
Now I perceive that she hath made compare
Between our statures; she hath urged her height;
And with her personage, her tall personage,
Her height forsooth, she hath prevail'd with him.
And are you grown so high in his esteem
Because I am so dwarfish and so low?
How low am I, thou painted maypole? Speak:
How low am I? I am not yet so low
But that my nails can reach unto thine eyes.

Hel.   I pray you, though you mock me, gentlemen,
Let her not hurt me....You perhaps may think,
Because she is something lower than myself,
That I can match her.

Her.   Lower'? Hark, again!

The term "puppet" is used as an insult.

Use quote marks to empasize being called a puppet.

Helena is tall — translation at this point needs to be straight-forward, but lead into 'high in his esteem.'

Be careful to match how these terms are used — "lower" must be signed the same way for both interpreters.

speech comparisons. uch sarcastic lection.

82

APPENDIX 5
LIST OF ADDITIONAL RESOURCES

Julie Gebron
c/o Butte Publications
P.O. Box 1328
Hillsboro, OR 97123-1328
jgeeadj@aol.com

Certified freelance intepreter and audio descriptor specializing in the arts. Presenter, workshop leader and consultant to theatres on issues of accessibility. Available to teach customized workshops on theatrical interpreting, education, access to the arts,etc.

Association for Theatre and Accessibililty
c/o Access Theatre   805-564-2063
527 Garden Street   805-564-2424 TTY
Santa Barbara, CA 93101   805-564-0051 FAX

International association which promotes accessibility to theatre. Maintains information files, actor resumes, publishes resource directory, newsletter and hosts an annual conference in August.

Theatre Development Fund (TDF) & Theatre Access Project (TAP)
1501 Broadway   212-221-0885
New York, NY 10030   212-768-1563 (FAX)

The Julliard School Evening Division
60 Lincoln Center Plaza   212-799-5040
New York, NY   212-799-5000 ext. 273

TDF and The Julliard School Evening Division co-sponsor courses on signing for the theatre. Specialized courses for proficient sign language interpreters who wish to enhance their skills by learning to interpret for the theatre. Classes offered during the school year for those living in the New York area. A summer training program is being considered. Approved sponsor of the RID CMP.

Hands On
131 Varick Street Room 909 212 627 4898 Voice
New York, NY 10013   212 627 1070 TTY
Web Page: http://HandsOn.org

Contact person: Beth Preover

Coordinate interpreted performances and publish monthly calender ofcultural events for the Deaf community. Information and referral. Theatrical interpreter training.

Kentucky Shakespeare Festival

1114 South Third Street   502-583-8738
Louisville, KY 40203   502-583-8751 (FAX)
Kyshakes@aol.com

Producing Director: Curt L. Tofteland

Offers intensive week long summer training in shadow interpreting with an emphasis on the plays of William Shakespeare and the Commedia dell 'Arte theatre.

Registry of Interpreters for the Deaf, Inc. (RID)

8719 Colesville Road, Suite 310   (301) 608-0050
Silver Spring, MD 20910-3919

Stagehands

c/o Special Audiences   404-892-1123 ext. 11 (voice)
1904 Monroe Drive   404-892-4208 (TTY)
Atlanta, GA 30324   404-872-8924 (FAX)

Stagehands coordinates ongoing theatrical interpreting for several theatres in Atlanta. Also provide interpreters for special events and museum tours. Training is sometimes offered; call for information.

Hartman and Hallet Interpreters

4428 Vandervork   612-925-2166
Edina, MN 55436-1431   612-929-3381 (TTY)

ATTN: Albert Walla

Refers interpreters for theatrical interpreting. Not currently offering training.

Theatrical Interpreting Project (TIP)

D.E.A.F.   612-297-6700
413 Wacouta Street
St. Paul, MN 55102

Planning to offer some training.

Glossary

APRON. The part of a proscenium stage in front of the curtain or proscenium arch; the "frame" around the stage. Also called the forestage.

ARENA. A configuration where the stage is surrounded by the audience. Also called "in-the-round" and "central staging".

ARTISTIC DIRECTOR. The person who sets the artistic path for a theatre company and oversees artistic aspects of production and design.

AUDITION. A try out where a speaking or signing actor performs a selected theater piece in front of a director. (An actor's job interview.)

BACKSTAGE. The area hidden from the audience's view behind the actual performing space. This includes the dressing rooms.

BLACKOUT. All house and stage lights are turned off, allowing actors to enter and exit, usually at the beginning and end of acts, and sometimes during scene changes.

BLOCKING. The movement of the actors on stage. Where, when and how the actors move about the stage as they enter, exit and cross.

BLOCKING REHEARSAL. A rehearsal in which actors, aided by the director, "set" or establish their stage movement.

BOOK. A script usually used in musical theatre.

BOOTH. See TECHNICAL or LIGHT BOOTH

BUSINESS. Acting movement connected with the handling of props, or merely any pantomimed action.

CALL. 1. The time an actor is expected at rehearsal or performance. 2. The warnings given by the stage manager before the performance to let the actors know how much time is left before the play will begin. Usually given at half hour before, then at fifteen minutes before, ten and five minutes before.

CALL BOARD. A bulletin board located backstage and/or near the stage door on which are posted important notices for actors and interpreters.

CATWALK. A narrow platform over the audience or above the fly space used by technicians for access to equuipment and rigging.

CHARACTERIZATION. The mannerisms, movements, actions, psychology and behaviors an actor uses to portray their character

"CLEAR THE STAGE." A command for all personell to leave the stage and remove all equipment and belongings. Also sometimes "strike the stage"

CLOSED REHEARSAL. A rehearsal whose attendance is by invitation only.

COMPS. A gratuity often awarded theatre artists, of free or "complimentary" tickets to a performance.

COUNTER. A slight movement to face a character who has just crossed you.

CROSS. To move to another location on the stage. If asked to "cross" another person, it means to move downstage until you have passed that person.

CUE. The words, signs, sounds, lighting or actions which precede your next action or line.

CUE-TO-CUE. A rehearsal during which tech elements are rehearsed merely by performing one cue, then jumping to the next cue.

CURTAIN CALL. The bowing of the actors at the end of the performance.

CUTS. Words or lines from the play which the director has deleted.

DESIGNER(S). Artists responsible for the technical elements used to present the director's vision for a production, such as costumes, lights, sets, hair, make-up, props.

DIRECTOR. The person responsible for presenting a written text and making it come alive on the stage.

DOWNSTAGE. The area at the front of the set, closest to the audience. Called downstage because sets used to be raked so that the back was higher than the front, so audiences could see better. *(See diagram at end of Glossary.)*

DRESS REHEARSAL. A full rehearsal of the play with costumes, and often with sets and lighting. Sometimes called a "dress/tech".

EQUITY. The actors union. Ensures safe and responsibly scheduled rehearsals and performances. Sets pay levels. Equity actors can only perform in Equity productions.

FIGHT DESIGNER/CHOREOGRAPHER/DIRECTOR. The person responsible for creating the fights/combat during a production, teaching the actors how to fight on stage without getting hurt.

FLAT. A wall of scenery

FLY. The high ceiling above most proscenium stages which allows sets and actors to "fly" in and out of view.

FOCUS. The object of the audience's attention.

FOURTH WALL. The set makes three sides of the "room," the FOURTH WALL is the imaginary side of the "room" which the audience looks through to view the play.

GELS. The transparent, colored plastic material used to cover stage lights to create various colors on the stage during performance.

GLOW TAPE. A glow-in-the-dark tape used to mark platform risers or other areas for use in blackouts.

GREEN ROOM. The resting area backstage for actors.

HEAD SHOT. A photograph, usually of the head and shoulders, used for publicity and promotion.

"HEADS UP." A warning to signal something is falling or being lowered from above. When called, each person should stop what they are doing and look up to see if they are in danger.

HOUSE. Technically this means the part of the theatre including the auditorium, box office, foyer and any other paces in front of the curtain or stage area. It is most commonly used to refer to the area where the audience is seated.

HOUSE LIGHTS. The lights specifically used before and after the show as well as at intermission, to allow the audience to find their seats and to read.

HOUSE TO HALF. The house lights are reduced in brightness by half, signaling that the show is beginning.

HOUSE TO BLACK. The house lights are completely extinguished in preparation for stage lighting as the show begins.

LIGHT BOARD. The electronic device used to raise and lower lights at designated times throughout the performance.

LINES. The actor's dialogue spoken during the play.

MASKING. Usually large black draperies (also called "blacks" or "tormentors and teasers") which hide backstage areas from audience view.

MOAT. The area in a raised proscenium separating the stage from the audience. Usually called the PIT.

MONOLOGUE. A dramatic soliloquy often performed alone on stage

NEUTRAL POSITION. A basic, unemotional stance; usually standing with feet comfortably shoulder width apart, hands at sides and head erect.

NON-EQUITY. A theatre that does not choose to join Actor's Equity. Theatres can set their own pay scales. Many local theatres are non-equity.

OFF BOOK. When lines are memorized.

ON BOOK. When someone is looking at the script to enable the memorization of lines.

ON DECK. To be the next person waiting to perform an act.

OPEN REHEARSAL. A rehearsal which anyone may attend without advanced permission. (Ask anyway.)

OPENING NIGHT. The official first night of performance with full costumes, lighting and set. Often attended by theatre reviewers.

PIT. Sunken area in front of the stage, also know as the "orchestra" and sometimes referred to as the "moat".

PLACES. The call given by the stage manager before the performance. It means, "Go to where you will make your first entrance."

PLATFORM INTERPRETING. Interpreters are placed in one stationary position during the performance, often to the side of the stage or below the apron.

PREVIEW. A rehearsal/performance with an audience present before the opening night.

PRODUCTION ASSISTANTS. The folks running around backstage, moving props, helping actors with costume changes, opening curtains and making sure everything is in the right place at the right time. Often seen wearing headsets and dressed in dark clothes.

PROJECT. To increase the volume of one's voice

PROSCENIUM. A configuration in which the audience all face an open frame in the wall which discloses the set, as if looking through a picture frame or watching a movie.

RAKE. 1. A set floor which angles down the further downstage it goes. 2. The angle of the set walls so that they come closer in the back, to aid the illusion of perspective.

REHEARSAL SPACE. The place where the play is rehearsed before actually moving into the theater. Usually a large open room.

RUN-THROUGH. A rehearsal of the show from beginning to end, usually the first or second time the show is rehearsed in entirety, without set, costumes or lighting.

SCRIIPT. The printed text of a play. TEXT is also used for script. The term BOOK is used more in musical theatre.

SET. The scenery, backdrops, and furnishings used to create or suggest a location and time period.

SHADOW INTERPRETING. A form of theatrical interpreting where the signing actors follow the blocking of the speaking actors, to maintain as close proximity as possible during the signed performance.

SIGHTLINES. The line of sight from the highest audience point and widest audience points, which together determine what is visible to the audience. A good sightline is where anyone sitting in the sightline can see the show well.

SIGN COACH. A person fluent in sign language, knowledgeable about theatre and able to assist with translation and feedback specific to signing for theatre.

SOUND BOARD. The electronic device through which sound is regulated and produced during the performance. It is usually located in the booth.

SPIKE. To mark the position of furniture or actors on stage, usually with tape.

STAGE DIRECTIONS. The terminology used to describe and notate actors movements on stage. *(See illustration at end of Glossary.)*

STAGE LEFT. The left side of the stage from the actor's perspective, facing the audience.

STAGE MANAGER. The person who runs the show after opening night and assists the director and actors during the rehearsal process. The stage manager is in complete charge of backstage, includingactors and crew.

STAGE RIGHT. The right side of the stage from the actor's perspective, facing the audience. *(See diagram at end of the Glossary.)*

STAND BY. A term meaning to be ready to perform an act as soon as the cue comes.

STEALING FOCUS. See UPSTAGING.

SUBTEXT. The unspoken feelings beneath the lines. What isn't being said.

TECHNICAL DIRECTOR. The person responsible for planning, organizing and supervising all production work, such as building a set.

TECHNICAL OR LIGHT BOOTH (the booth). An enclosed booth where the stage manager and technical personnel sit during the performance, adding sound effects, lighting and directing production assistants.

TEXT. A script.

THRUST OR MODIFIED THRUST. A stage which physically extends outward into the audience so that some of the seating area surrounds part of the stage. A modified thrust is not so deeply extended into the audience.

TRAP. An opening in the floor which allows access from below the stage.

UPSTAGING. When one's actions, position or movement takes focus from the actor whom the audience should be watching. Also called "stealing focus".

VOMITORIUM (VOM). Aisleways emerging from beneath the audience used for entrances and exits.

"WALK THE SET". To physically walk about on a finished set to familiarize yourself with its layout. This is before the audience is allowed into the theatre.

WARM UPS. Exercises (mental, physical and vocal) used before the show to enable the actor to be prepared for the performance.

WINGS. The offstage areas where actors wait before their entrances; usually refers to the areas immediately to the left and right of the stage.

ZONE INTERPRETING. Interpreters are placed in designated areas on the stage interpreting for actors as they move within the selected "zone" of the interpreter.

Diagram of Stage Directions

BACKSTAGE

UPSTAGE

Up Right	Up Right Center	Up Left Center	Up Left
Stage Right	Right Center	Left Center	Stage Left
Down Right	Down Right Center	Down Left Center	Down Left

STAGE RIGHT

STAGE LEFT

DOWNSTAGE

AUDIENCE